# Secret Techniques for Controlling Your Fear, Anxiety, Sadness, Anger, and Other Unwanted Emotions

### By Vlad Koros

Text Copyright © 2012 Vladislav Korostyshevskiy

All Rights Reserved

ISBN-13: 978-1503259942

ISBN-10: 1503259943

INTRODUCTION: WHY CONTROL YOUR EMOTIONS?..................................................................11

CHAPTER 1: EXPERIENCING EMOTIONS IN THE BODY..................................................................................17

Feelings' Locations in the Body....................................25

Disgust..............................................................................26

Sadness.............................................................................28

Joy.....................................................................................29

Aversion...........................................................................30

Fear...................................................................................31

Anger................................................................................32

Anxiety.............................................................................33

Sexual Desire...................................................................34

Stronger and Weaker Feelings of the Same Kind.......35

Disgust..............................................................................35

Sadness.............................................................................37

Joy.....................................................................................38

Aversion...........................................................................39

Fear...................................................................................40

Anger................................................................................42

Anxiety.............................................................................43

Sexual Desire...................................................................44

When Emotions Spill Out of Their Containers....................44

Summary.............................................................................46

CHAPTER 2: EMOTIONS AND THE ACTIVATING BREATH.............................................................................50

Bodily Imagination.............................................................52

The Activating Inhalation...................................................55

Exercise: Introduction to Intervening in Activating Inhalation............................................................................58

Breathing with Your Chest..................................................61

Exercise: Intervening in Sadness Formation.......................62

Exercise: Intervening in Aversion Formation.....................64

Breathing with Your Upper Abdomen.................................65

Exercise: Intervening in Anger Formation..........................66

Exercise: Intervening in Anxiety Formation.......................69

Exercise: Intervening in Fear Formation............................73

Breathing with Your Lower Abdomen................................74

Exercise: Intervening in Disgust Formation.......................76

Exercise: Intervening in Activation of Sexual Desire............78

The Relative Intensity of Emotions....................................79

Cascading Situations...........................................................84

Summary.............................................................................87

CHAPTER 3: EMOTIONS AND

MOVEMENTS OF THE TORSO..................................................90

Technique 1: Basic Suppression.......................................93

Joy..................................................................................94

Exercise: Disruption of Joy................................................95

Aversion..........................................................................96

Exercise: Disruption of Aversion........................................98

Sadness...........................................................................100

Exercise: Disruption of Sadness.......................................101

Anxiety............................................................................103

Exercise: Disruption of Anxiety........................................104

Anger..............................................................................106

Exercise: Disruption of Anger..........................................107

Fear.................................................................................108

Exercise: Disruption of Fear.............................................109

Disgust.............................................................................110

Exercise: Disruption of Disgust........................................111

Sexual Desire...................................................................112

Exercise: Disruption of Sexual Desire...............................113

**Technique 2**: Forceful Suppression............................114

Joy..................................................................................116

Exercise: Disruption of Joy...............................................116

Aversion..................................................................117

Exercise: Disruption of Aversion...............................118

Sadness..................................................................119

Exercise: Disruption of Sadness................................119

Anxiety..................................................................120

Exercise: Disruption of Anxiety................................121

Anger.....................................................................122

Exercise: Disruption of Anger...................................123

Fear........................................................................124

Exercise: Disrupting the Formation of Fear...................124

Disgust...................................................................126

Exercise: Disruption of Disgust.................................126

Sexual Desire..........................................................127

**Technique 3**: Release of Pressure............................128

Joy.........................................................................129

Naturally Occurring Disruption of Joy.......................129

Exercise: Disruption of Joy......................................130

Aversion.................................................................132

Naturally Occurring Disruption of Aversion................133

Exercise: Disruption of Aversion...............................134

Sadness..................................................................135

Naturally Occurring Disruption of Sadness……………..136

Exercise: Disruption of Sadness…………………………136

Anxiety…………………………………………………..138

Naturally Occurring Disruption of Anxiety……………..138

Exercise: Disruption of Anxiety…………………………139

Fear……………………………………..……………..141

Naturally Occurring Disruption of Fear………………...142

Exercise: Disruption of Fear……………………………..142

Disgust…………………………………………………..144

Naturally Occurring Disruption of Disgust……………...144

Exercise: Disruption of Disgust…………………………145

Sexual Desire…………………………………………...146

Naturally Occurring Disruption of the Sexual Desire…….147

Summary………………………………………………148

CHAPTER 4: EMOTIONS AND GOAL SETTING……..152

What Keeps the Dream Alive?...........................................153

The Goal-Setting Process………………………...……157

Technique 1: Halting the Push…………………………...160

Exercise: Turning Off Feelings Using a Dummy Goal….164

Alternative Approach to Technique 1: Turning off Feelings without a Goal..…………………………….…..166

Getting to Know Your Mind Sight……………………..167

Exercise: Letting Your Mind Spin…………………....169

Technique 2: Giving the Push from the Back a Boost…..170

Getting to Know the Boost…………………………..171

Exercise: Using the Boost to Turn Any Emotion into Satisfaction……………………………………………172

Technique 3: Redirecting the Push along an

Alternative Route……………………..………………174

Getting to Know Your Stubbornness……………….176

Exercise: Being Stubborn . . . on Purpose……………178

Technique 4: Controlling the Push

Using Facial Expression……………………………179

Getting to Know the Relationship

between the Push and Facial Expressions……………182

Exercise: Turning Off Feelings

Using a Facial Expression……………………………185

Summary…………………………………………...187

CHAPTER 5: EMOTIONS AND

THE SECOND BREATH……………………………192

Natural Occurrence of the Phenomenon

behind the Technique………………………………194

Essential Components of the Technique………………201

Intensity of Muscle Tension..................................202

Higher-Quality Breathing......................................203

Pelvic Alignment..................................................204

Joy......................................................................206

The Natural Occurrence of Joy.............................207

Exercise: Disruption of Joy..................................207

Aversion............................................................209

The Natural Occurrence of Aversion.......................210

Exercise: Disruption of Aversion............................210

Sadness.............................................................211

The Natural Occurrence of Sadness........................212

Exercise: Disruption of Sadness.............................213

Anxiety..............................................................214

The Natural Occurrence of Anxiety.........................215

Exercise: Disruption of Anxiety..............................216

Anger.................................................................218

The Natural Occurrence of Anger...........................219

Exercise: Disruption of Anger................................220

Fear...................................................................221

The Natural Occurrence of Fear.............................222

Exercise: Disruption of Fear..................................222

Disgust……………………………………………..224

The Natural Occurrence of Disgust……………………225

Exercise: Disruption of Disgust……………………..225

Sexual Desire……………………………………..227

The Natural Occurrence of Sexual Desire……………..227

Exercise: Disruption of Sexual Desire…………………228

Summary……………………………………...…229

# INTRODUCTION: WHY CONTROL YOUR EMOTIONS?

One day, Caroline M.—a longtime patient of my acupuncture practice—complained to me that ever since her husband had left her, she had been having the sensation of a hole in the middle of her upper abdomen. Recently this sensation had become stronger and was bothering her a lot.

"Would you like to get rid of it?" I asked her.

"I already tried distracting myself from it with various things, but that didn't work," she replied.

"What I'm suggesting," I said, "is that you learn some techniques for controlling your feelings. You won't need to distract yourself from the emotions that bother you, or repress them, or anything of that sort. And you can do these techniques all by yourself. Using the same mechanisms that brought the unwanted feeling about, you can simply turn it off."

Caroline, whom I was treating for stiffness in her neck, didn't mention her sensation again during the acupuncture session—until the very end, that is. Before leaving, she turned around and said to me, "We're human, you know. What would happen if we stopped having feelings?"

"Caroline, you're making too much of it. Your feelings won't go away—after all, emotions are part of our nature. But you'd be able to modify or eliminate those feelings that bother you."

"I don't know, but it sounds wrong," she said on her way out.

That was not the first time that someone had reacted this way when I'd suggested they learn how to deliberately control their emotions, and yet I'm always amazed at how defensive people are about their feelings. Why are we so protective of our emotions?

It seems that even bad emotions create a sense of comfort—false comfort, that is. And you can tell that the comfort that emotions provide is false because when you turn a feeling off, you experience a much greater comfort—the kind that comes from satisfaction, the feeling of relief.

Feelings are often inconvenient and counterproductive. Think about it: Suppose you are thinking of going back to school part time to further you career, but there's an emotional obstacle. You know that you really hate to study. You don't want to have to do homework or to spend your off-hours attending classes or reading boring textbooks or to worry about your grades or upcoming tests. In such a case, would it be so wrong to turn your reluctance *off*?

Learning to reset your emotions isn't as unnatural as you might think. The techniques that I describe in this book are, in fact, derived from the tricks that our minds instinctively use to control the emotional aspects of our lives. The crucial difference between what occurs naturally and what we can do using the techniques extracted from our instincts is that, in the majority of instances, our natural tendency is to *repress* our feelings, while the methods explained in this book are aimed at *turning our emotions off.* Interestingly enough, our impulse to defend our feelings is essentially what prevents our minds from naturally dissolving unwanted emotions fully.

In great many cases, you do not need to turn off your feelings completely in order to experience sufficient relief; oftentimes, all you need to do is to steer your emotions onto another course. For example, say that you have been married for twenty years, and many little things that your spouse does—which you initially found endearing—now irritate you more and more with each passing day! Of course, some people in such a situation would choose to get a divorce, but if those little things are the only reason you and your spouse cannot stay together, wouldn't you rather try to reset your emotional patterns? Admittedly, it would be extremely difficult to reset your emotional makeup to the condition it was in when you'd just gotten married, but you can form a new emotional state by tweaking the feelings you already have. It may even be enough simply to release some of the emotional pressure that has accumulated over the years of married life.

This certainly is the case with stress. Just picture yourself having been working hard for a year and desperately needing a vacation. But why do you need a vacation? Most likely, all you need is to relieve some of the stress that has come from working so hard. But what if you adjusted your emotional response so you were not as stressed out? Would that be wrong? Would it make you less human? Curiously, if you were to take a vacation purely for fun and not because you *had* to get away, you would be able to enjoy it on a whole different level.

And there's another problem with emotions—one that's very deep seated. Our emotions are often unconnected to any present reality. For instance, you may be a healthy, relatively young person with a loving family and lots of friends, but you find yourself troubled by thoughts of being sick, old, and alone. Notice that it is not the thoughts themselves that are troubling, but rather the emotional response that they trigger in you. These feelings might be part of the emotional foundation your entire life—always in the back of your mind, even when you're distracted by more immediate concerns, and constantly influencing the formation of your other feelings and, consequently, your actions. Would it make you less human if you reduced the burden of this emotionally troubling mindset?

Caroline M. came back after four months for another acupuncture treatment for her neck stiffness. "Can you still show me those exercises that are supposed to make that hole disappear?" she asked me unexpectedly.

"Yes, sure. But what changed your mind?"

"Apparently my body found a solution to that problem: It makes me eat. I've gained 15 pounds! Now I don't feel good. I get tired quicker. This is not a normal weight for me, and I've got to try to make this hole disappear."

I taught Caroline a few of the techniques included in this book, but the technique of manipulating the activating breath (covered in chapter 2) was enough to solve her problem. Within two weeks, she learned to control the sensation of having a hole in her upper abdomen, and her weight returned to normal in three months.

This book explains seven different approaches to achieving the same goal: disruption of the formation of unwanted feelings. A last, eighth approach describes how to turn *on* an emotion—either because you want or need it or to restore a feeling that you've mistakenly deactivated. Because all these techniques deal with the same phenomenon of emotional formation and the mechanisms by which our minds and bodies switch or cancel feelings, you can choose the technique or techniques that suit you best. After all, the purpose of the book is to give you more choices regarding how to deal with your feelings. And the choices themselves remain yours.

Living among other people requires you to suppress your emotions frequently, which means that repressing emotions is as much part of being human as is experiencing feelings. If that's true, then doesn't intentional control of your emotions make you a more evolved human being? I'll let you decide.

## CHAPTER 1: EXPERIENCING EMOTIONS IN THE BODY

Let's imagine that a woman—we'll call her Mary Ann—is considering buying an apartment. We see her sitting at her dining room table, calculating her prospective expenses. The apartment she's thinking of buying is not very big, but it is located in a quiet neighborhood and is just a 30-minute train ride away from her job. "It's a good investment," Mary Ann keeps saying to herself. "It has enough space for me for now, and it should be easy to sell later on."

But, to be honest, Mary Ann has her heart set on a different apartment—a penthouse in a large building that has a pool, a gym, a garage, and a doorman. She could not resist taking a tour of that penthouse two days ago, despite knowing very well that she could not afford it. As Mary Ann thinks about the penthouse, she stops calculating and looks up. Staring at the wall, she imagines herself in those sumptuous living quarters, and she feels that she already owns the penthouse. She sees herself sitting in a comfortable chair in the huge living room, watching a movie on a large-screen television set. The 600 square feet of the apartment she is currently renting suffocate her, and the air in the imagined penthouse seems fresher. The views of the city from her living room, bedroom, and kitchen are magnificent. She knows just what she'd do with the place. In one of its two bathrooms, Mary Ann would install a hot tub, and she'd put a Jacuzzi in the other. She leans back in her chair, dreaming of the life in her new apartment. And while she is daydreaming, let us discover where her feelings are coming from by observing her body language.

When Mary Ann was doing her calculations, she was stooped over her table and notebook. But as soon as she thought of her dream apartment, she lifted her head. Sinking deeper into her daydream, Mary Ann straightened her torso and she leaned back in her chair. We saw a smile appear on her face, and noticed that the middle of her torso, where her chest and abdomen come together, arched forward slightly. There's nothing unusual about Mary Ann's actions: we all move this way when we daydream.

Think of a time when *you* wanted something. It doesn't have to be something big, but it should be something that you wanted intensely—and something that you got. As soon as the mental image of that object appears in your mind's eye, do you feel a push in the middle of your back, above your waist and below the lower edges of your shoulder blades, which compels you to straighten your back and to arch your upper abdomen slightly forward? If your desire is strong enough, you will feel the urge to stand up and walk around. A desire of great intensity seems to push you to go straight toward your goal. Now, try to remember what happened when you got the thing you wanted. Try to recall how your desire disappeared. That feeling of desire disappearing is what we call *satisfaction*.

Many of your desires, however, are never satisfied or are satisfied only to a degree. Whether the reasons are external obstacles or your own conflicting wishes, that initial push from the back becomes dispersed in your body, giving rise to increased muscle tension.

But let us return to Mary Ann. She is in the middle of her daydream when she remembers that she cannot afford her dream apartment. Her smile disappears and she once again stoops over the notebook, using her body to hamper that push from the back that helped form her daydream.

Before leaving Mary Ann, let's notice one interesting aspect of her story. Her desire for the penthouse apartment—and her daydreaming about it—were, in fact, a waste of time. Her desire moved her no closer to her goal, and her daydreaming may even have been counterproductive, in the sense that she felt bad when she "woke up" to the fact that the penthouse was unaffordable. She would have been in better shape had she actually controlled her mind—and her emotions. The daydream of owning the penthouse momentarily pacified some of her feelings—her dissatisfaction with her living arrangements, her restlessness in her current home—but those feelings returned strongly as soon as the daydream was over.

"Controlling" your mind may seem like tricking yourself into believing that you have what you want even when you do not have it. But that's not what I mean. I'm talking about the recognition that, in reality, there is very little connection between *wishing* for something and actually *having* it.

It's true in a sense that your feelings act as messengers between you and everything else in the world, but it's also true that there is an abyss between your wishes and the surrounding physical world. Not only can't wishing for something bring it into being, but feelings are often complicated in ways that have nothing to do with external reality. For example, Mary Ann does not want to buy an apartment simply because she wants it. She wants to buy an apartment because she believes that owning her own home would resolve some of her feelings. She might feel safer living in her own place, or more "adult" and responsible, or she might just like the sense of ownership, but buying an apartment would only change Mary Ann's feelings and *nothing else.* And, as paradoxical as it may sound, were Mary Ann able to control her feelings and *not* want to buy an apartment anymore, she would be able to make a better choice about which home to buy, or she might even come up with an idea about where to find additional resources to buy her dream home, because her feelings would not have clouded her judgment.

This *clouding of judgment* is a frequent problem when we are experiencing emotions: our feelings reset the boundaries of our thought processes and often rob us of many possible choices that we potentially have in our lives. Think about it: Suppose you have finally found the time and means to visit a museum that you have wanted to visit, but as soon as you arrive, you begin feeling hungry and really cannot fully appreciate what you see around you. Of course, you can go to the museum cafeteria for a bite to eat—but that's not the reason you came to the museum, and it will steal some of your time there. Your hunger has clouded your judgment.

"Wait a second," you are probably thinking. "Since when has hunger become a *feeling*?" Well, it is a feeling in the sense meant in this book. And here is why:

How do you recognize that you are hungry? You feel something in your upper abdomen, as if there were a hole inside your solar plexus. What compels you to look for food, however, is not this sensation alone. It is also the emotional response—which in this case is a form of panic—that you develop as a reaction to the sensation. So do you want to follow your so-called instinct and search for food, or would you rather—given the choice—turn it off for a couple of hours and take a look around the museum, instead?

A friend of mine once told me that she got married to first her husband because she felt desperate—all her girlfriends were getting married, and she was the only one without a husband. She and her husband divorced after fifteen years, but that is not the biggest problem. The biggest problem is that those fifteen years of her life were based on her desperation, which I am sure was the background feeling during her entire marriage. Would it have been so wrong if my friend, had she known how to control her feelings, had eliminated her desperation and instead used a pleasant emotion as a guide in her search for the right husband? The feeling of desperation is another form of panic—and therefore similar to the emotional response to feeling hungry. How do I know that? Because the areas of my body in which I experience the sensations that my mind interprets as panic are the same in situations in which I feel hungry and in which I feel desperate. And the areas in the body where emotions occur are the same for everybody, which you will be able confirm from your own observations. This is the basis for the method that I am offering you in this book, which in a nutshell is this:

All the emotions that you can possibly experience in your life, you experience *in your body*. Every emotion is a combination of sensations that your mind instantly and without the slightest hesitation translates into a feeling. All the techniques described in this book are aimed at the sensations that constitute emotion. As you modify those sensations, your feelings will either change or vanish. The techniques that I am about to explain are not invented; they are the tricks that your mind naturally uses to regulate your emotional state. You will be able to identify these tricks as you observe the behavior of your own mind as you imagine the fictitious or real-life situations that I will be offering throughout this book. When you identify the mechanisms your mind uses to regulate your emotional reactions, you will be able to take conscious control of your feelings consciously. This will require some practice, but anyone can do it.

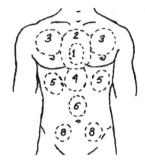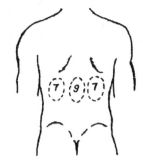

**Figure 1.** There are eight distinct areas in your body where you feel specific emotions:

(1) joy,             (5) anger,

(2) aversion,    (6) disgust,

(3) sadness,     (7) fear,

(4) anxiety,     (8) sexual desire.

Behind and between the areas that contain fear is the area in which the push that always accompanies daydreams and reinforces every feeling originates (9).

## Feelings' Locations in the Body

As Figure 1 shows, there are eight distinct areas, or "containers," in your body where you feel specific emotions. Do not think of these containers as internal organs, but rather as discrete physical spaces within the torso where emotions are felt. (Again, you'll be able to confirm this for yourself as you perform the exercises in this book.) Of course, emotional states go by many different names, but for simplicity's sake let's use the following common names for emotions as we identify their locations in the body: (1)

disgust, (2) sadness, (3) joy, (4) aversion, (5) fear, (6) anger, (7) anxiety, and (8) sexual desire.

## Disgust

I remember a time when an undergraduate biology class I was in took a field trip to a medical school. When we arrived, a medical school administrator gave us a two-hour lecture on what we should expect from a job in healthcare and how to prepare for it. After the lecture, we had lunch. When we had just finished eating, the administrator announced that we were going to see a dissection. Being biology students, we had cut our share of frogs and rats, and seeing or even participating in a dissection was no longer a big deal. But once we entered the anatomy lab, we all stopped. There were eleven operating stations, each with a human cadaver on it.

I'm not sure how many of us had ever seen a dead person before. As the thick smell of formaldehyde tickled our noses, we stood by the entrance with grimaces of disgust on our faces and shock in our eyes. Our biology professor accompanied us into the lab, introducing himself and the entire class to the medical-school anatomy professor, who was sitting at his desk eating a sandwich.

We quietly followed our professor around the lab, from one dissecting station to another, while he explained what the medical-school students were doing. As we were touching the grayish-green, formaldehyde-soaked tissues of a cadaver, one of my classmates threw up, and another had to step outside until his stomach calmed down.

One of the students asked the professor a question that he did not know how to answer, and so he called to the anatomy instructor for help. The anatomy professor walked over to where we were, eating his sandwich. He listened to the student's question, nodded, put his half-eaten sandwich on top of the cadaver, and lifted the surprisingly thick, incised skin of the dead man. I heard several stomachs rumble around me. The semi-transparent fascia stretched like a spider's web, exposing a layer of muscles. The anatomy professor did not bother putting on gloves—touching, spreading, and pulling with his bare hands. When he finished his explanation, he took his sandwich and hungrily resumed consuming what was left of it. Two more classmates had to leave the room.

The reason I am telling you this unpleasant story is to make it clear that we experience feelings *in our bodies*—specifically, in our torsos. That's easy to see in the case of the feeling of disgust, which can make us nauseated. But it's just as true of any other feeling. No feeling ever originates in the head, legs, or arms. This is crucial to understand if you want to learn to control your feelings. Feelings are identified by their locations in our bodies.

The container of disgust, for instance, occupies the center of your abdomen. Its lower boundary is located about one finger's-breadth above your navel, and the container's front wall extends about four finger's-breadths upward; the back (interior) wall of the container extends a bit farther up—about five finger's-breadths above the navel line at its deepest boundary, which is behind your stomach.

**Sadness**

To understand emotions' containers better, let's consider another scenario. Chris had been with his girlfriend for five years, but just a few minutes ago they had a terrible fight and broke up. She told him, "Never call me again!" Now, Chris is slowly walking down an empty street, slouching, stepping heavily, sighing a lot, and almost crying—not just because they'd been together all that time, but because they were in love! Even without knowing what just happened to Chris, you can see that he is sad. But why are you so sure about it? Well, just from the way he looks. You don't even have to think about it; you understand it immediately despite the fact that you did not witness the argument between Chris and his girlfriend.

If you think of several sad situations from your past, you'll notice that you recognize sadness by a heavy sensation in your chest. You assume that everybody else feels sadness in his or her chest, too, and your assumption is correct.

**Joy**

Now, let's imagine that, despite all their differences, Chris and his girlfriend have made up, because they still *do* love each other. Now we again see Chris walking down the street, but his chest is no longer caved in and his back is no longer slouched. In fact, quite the opposite is true: his chest is bulging, his step seems lighter, and I believe there's a smile on his face. I think you would agree that Chris looks happy. And his happiness seems to concentrate in his chest, just as his sadness did. Yet the difference is enormous!

If you want to identify what exactly the difference is, recall any situation in which you felt joy. You felt it in your chest, yes? Now recall a sad situation from your past, and run it back to back with the joyous one. Do you feel the difference? Each of these feelings has a very specific "pocket," or container, in your body, in which it suddenly appears whenever a situation activates it. The pockets for sadness and joy are both in the chest, but in different locales. Sadness appears in the sides of your chest, while joy appears in the center.

**Aversion**

Once, when my friends Angela and Peter's son Justin was still a toddler, I stopped by their house and witnessed the following scene: Angela was trying to feed Justin, but he did not want to eat. Every time the spoon came near Justin's mouth, he shook his head, made faces, and whined. Little Justin's unwillingness to eat was an instance of an emotion we'll call *aversion*.

Imagine that you have to go to the movies with friends, because you made a promise, but for some reason you really do not want to go. You've probably been in such a situation: Maybe you didn't want to go because you hate the kind of movie you were supposed to see, or you were tired, or there was a program on television that you really wanted to watch. Recall that situation to mind—just as if it were happening now—and try to identify what makes you so sure that you do not want to go. What do you feel—and where do you feel it? It's the same feeling of aversion that Justin experienced, and you—like anyone—will also feel it around the center of the chest, enclosing the container of joy. And even though you are not a child anymore, you do feel the urge to shake your head and whine. (Making faces goes without saying—what sane person does not like to do that?)

### Fear

You've probably heard the expression "stopped like a deer in the headlights" or perhaps even had a chance to witness such a reaction. But why does fright trigger a state of temporary paralysis?

Imagine that you are walking along a dark road, when a car appears from around the corner and is speeding straight at you! What sensations do you experience and where do you feel them?

You should feel a pressure-like sensation in your back, below each of your shoulder blades but above your waist—this is where the containers of fear are located. Do you also feel how these sensations noticeably paralyze you? This paralysis occurs because the containers of fear block the push from your back—the same push that helps to form your daydreams. This push is also a crucial component in the formation of all the goals that you set and the movements you make. Because you need it to act in response to the fast-approaching car but the activated fear containers block the push, your ability to react seems to be temporarily turned off.

**Anger**

Imagine that you're in a coffee shop working on your brand-new laptop. You have to go to the bathroom, and so you do—leaving the computer on the table. You're gone for only a few minutes, but when you return . . . your expensive new computer has vanished! You ask the other patrons if they saw anything, but they all just shake their heads. You check with the people behind the counter, but they, too, deny seeing anything. You can't believe it. Someone stole your computer, nobody seems to care, and you are enraged! Imagine that intense anger. (But don't get too upset. You can have your imaginary computer back in a moment.)

Now think about where and how you feel this anger. What you feel is a pressure, directed inwardly, in a fist-sized spot on the each side of your ribcage, halfway between the flanks' midlines and the center of your upper abdomen. These are the containers of anger.

Activation of all the emotions described so far begins as a pressure sensation in the corresponding containers. There is one container, however, where the sensation is manifested differently. That's the container of anxiety.

**Anxiety**

Imagine that you are about to take an important test. Passing it can have a significant impact on your future, and despite feeling prepared, you still are worried. Now observe your torso: How do you know that you are worried? Where do you feel the sensations that your mind unhesitatingly recognizes as anxiety? You always feel them in the solar plexus, but notice what the sensations are: At the very beginning, when anxiety's container is just being activated, you feel a pressure deep in the middle of your upper abdomen, but then it almost immediately disappears, turning into weakness. The whole area of solar plexus begins to tremble, and it does not seem to support your upper body as well as it does when you are not feeling anxious. So, when you experience anxiety—whether subtle or full blown—you do not feel pressure. On the contrary, the whole container seems to dissolve. There is one more area, however, that behaves even more strangely.

**Sexual Desire**

Imagine that Bill, a high school student, likes his classmate Christine. Every time they talk, his heart beats faster and louder, and his voice trembles. Once, when he saw Christine going into a movie theater with some other classmates, Bill felt angry and upset. When Bill found out that Christine would be going away to college after graduation, he became sad. He feared that he might never see her again.

So what is going on here? Well, think about any situation when you were sexually attracted to someone. You feel slight pressure in two spots about a hand's-width to each side and about three finger-breadths down from your navel, but the area does not constrict—it expands. You see, sexual desire, which in a way is a feeling, resets your mind to a different mode. And in that mode, *any* container can become active, which means that you can experience any emotion. In fact, any feeling that you experience when you're in this mode feels particularly sharp.

## Stronger and Weaker Feelings of the Same Kind

Whenever you experience a feeling, you will also experience other sensations that are not directly related to that feeling but which appear along with it. To be able to tell which sensations are relevant to the emotion that you wish to change, you need to identify the sensations that comprise that particular feeling by observing how the feeling naturally appears. You will remember all those sensations that your feelings (or at least the major ones) consist of much better if you compare two degrees of each individual feeling: one when the feeling is mild and the other when the feeling becomes strong.

**Disgust**

Imagine that your vacation is about to start—the two glorious weeks of rest! You have carefully planned every single step of the trip that you'd booked, so not an hour of your vacation would be wasted. But, as it often happens, right before you are supposed to leave, your whole carefully planned set of actions is turning into a hurry. You still managed to compose yourself and stuck to your plan. The entire vacation has passed like a wonderful dream, with the exception of a strange feeling that you forgot something. Now you are coming home—as painful as it is, but vacations usually do end—and when you open the door to your home, a powerful, sickening stench hits you like an explosion. (Try to imagine the degree of the disgust that you are feeling.) As you enter the kitchen, you suddenly know what's creating the stink—and what it was you forgot to do. The night before you'd left for vacation, you'd made fried chicken, and you'd thrown the parts you didn't use in the garbage, . . . which you never bothered to take out!

But that raw chicken didn't just go bad—oh, no! As you look inside the garbage can, you see that it is covered with little, wiggling white worms. Ugh! (Do not panic; we will clean everything up in a minute.)

As you imagine this scenario, carefully compare the difference in the sensation you felt in reaction to the disgusting smell to the sensation you felt when you saw the chicken covered with maggots in the trash. You initially feel the pressure in the depth of your mid-abdomen, about a finger's-breadth above your navel. Then, when you see the rotting chicken, this sensation momentarily fills the container of disgust width-wise and travels toward the front surface of your body, then moves upward along the walls of the container, reaching and squeezing the lower half of your stomach. All the possible degrees of disgust follow this pattern when spreading within the container of disgust.

**Sadness**

Imagine that your best friend is taking a job in a different country for one year. (As you do, try to remember the sensations that indicate sadness to you.) Then imagine that after that year has passed, you find out that your friend has decided to stay in the foreign country indefinitely. That makes you wonder whether you will ever meet again, making you feel even sadder.

In both cases you feel sadness in the sides of your chest, but what changes about the sensation when your sadness intensifies? The sensations that we interpret as sadness start out in each of the two lower points of the containers of sadness, deep in your torso, at the line where your chest is connected to your upper abdomen. From the start, these sensations feel heavy. When you think that your friend will be away for only one year, this heaviness remains on the bottoms of the containers (well, unless you are really sentimental!). But when you find out that your best friend may never come back, the heaviness spreads forward and backward, filling the containers in the same fashion a bucket gets filled with water: moving upward only when it reaches the boundaries of the containers on each side. How much of the containers gets activated depends on your particular reaction, but the way in which they fill with sadness always remains the same.

## Joy

Imagine that you work for a large corporation. Business is going really well, so your boss lets you know that you will be getting an extra week of vacation. Isn't it lovely? But then your boss tells you another piece of news: You are getting a raise, too! (Hey, this is your imagination; if you cannot get what you want here, then where?) Getting more vacation days is exciting, and then getting more money on top of the extra vacation time is even better. As the good news piles up, what changes in the sensations that your mind interprets as joy? And how do you know that your joy is increasing?

The feeling of joy always occupies the very center of your chest. When you heard about the additional vacation days, you felt a light, bubbly sensation appearing at the bottom of the container. Then, when you found out about the raise, this sensation filled the container, moving upward. Joy fills out its container the same way sadness does—first filling it wall to wall and only then moving upward—but joy's container is much more narrow, so the way in which the container fills is not as obvious, because it happens quicker.

**Aversion**

Imagine that you're at work and need to finish a project as soon as possible. You really do not feel like staying after work, but you think you'll be able to complete the project in a couple of hours, so it shouldn't be too bad. After a few hours, though, it's clear that you won't be able to finish and that you will have to come back during the weekend. You really do not feel like coming to work on your day off, but, unfortunately, the job must be done!

Now, carefully compare your reluctance to stay at work for a few more hours with the feeling you experience when it's clear you'll have to come into the office over the weekend. Both feelings appear in and stay within the same container—the container of aversion—in the middle of your chest. (Remember: the container of aversion encloses that of joy.) But the expectation of staying for only a couple of hours causes a twirling sensation deeper in your chest, while the prospect of working on the weekend makes this twirling move closer to the front surface of your torso, intensifying your feeling of aversion.

**Fear**

Imagine you are at home alone, late at night, and all of a sudden you hear a loud thump in the next room. What do you feel? Startled, undoubtedly—you feel a rush of fear in the back of your ribcage. Try to hold the sensation of that fear in your imagination for a moment.

Now, imagine a different scenario. You and your friends are having a picnic in the woods. As you're setting up the lunch, you realize that you've forgotten to take the napkins out of your bag, and you reach behind yourself—not looking at the bag—to get them. As you do, you find yourself touching something that does *not* feel like your bag. That something makes a sudden hissing sound, and as you turn to see what it is, you see a flash of movement and feel a sharp, piercing pain! A large snake has just bitten your forearm and is quickly slithering away! What do you feel? Intense fright—so intense that you might call it *shock*.

Imagine yourself in this situation. Where do you feel this fear, and what is its quality like, as opposed to the fear you experienced when you heard the thump at night? You feel it in your back, deep inside your ribcage, in about the same place that you felt the fear when you were startled by the thump. But you'll notice that the differences between these two fears have to do with their intensity and continuity. The fear triggered by the loud thump is less intense, and it starts and stays near the core of your torso—the area closer to the solar plexus. The fear triggered by the snakebite, by contrast, is much greater. It fills its entire pocket to the brim, meaning it's very intense, making your whole body feel noticeably numb.

If you think of several situations that have triggered your fear, you will notice that different situations produce fears of different intensities. Fear's location is always the same place in the body—in the back, deep within the ribcage between the waist and under each of the lower edges of the shoulder blades. But notice the pattern of its movement. Fear starts out closer to the core of your torso and then spreads in the backward direction, first filling the whole container wall to wall and only then progressing toward the back's surface.

**Anger**

Imagine that you are writing something by hand, when your pen runs out of ink. Hold that mild irritation in your imagination for a moment.

Now imagine that you are typing something important on your computer, and your computer crashes. In both cases, you feel irritation, but the empty pen triggers a lesser aggravation than the broken computer does. But how do you tell the difference? In both cases, you feel sensations in the containers of anger, but the irritation caused by the empty pen is marked by pressure and tingling closer to the upper abdomen's surface, while the anger produced by the broken computer extends deeper into your body, outlining large portions of the containers.

**Anxiety**

Imagine that you have an examination scheduled for a week from now. You feel a little bit worried. Now imagine that the week has passed and the test is about to start. Your anxiety has become much stronger. What are the changes in sensation that indicate to you that your anxiety has become stronger? A week before the exam, you felt trembling deep inside your solar plexus. As the date of the test comes closer, this vibration seems to spread toward the surface of your upper abdomen. As with other emotions, the sensation of anxiety first fills the container wall to wall—from the top boundary under your chest down to the upper portion of your stomach, and to the sides where it touches the containers of anger—before it moves forward to the front surface of the torso.

**Sexual Desire**

First think of someone whom you find mildly sexually attractive. Hold the sensations that you are feeling in your memory for a moment, and then think of somebody whom you find extremely sexually desirable.

The first sensations of sexual desire appear near the surface of your lower abdomen, in two small areas, one on either side of your body, about a hand's-width sideways and two finger's-breadths down from your navel. When you think about the person whom you find very desirable, the sensations that start at those two points spread deeper into your body moving directly toward your back, until they reach the container's wall, and then they move up, engulfing other containers and resetting them in relation to the mental object that triggered these sensations. You may even feel your heart skipping a beat when the active sex-drive area naturally paralyzes the container of aversion and takes over the container of joy.

## When Emotions Spill Out of Their Containers

The containers of emotions do not "stretch." As feelings become stronger, they fill greater portions of their corresponding containers. But when an emotion gets too strong, the emotion "spills out" of its container.

Disgust. When the container of disgust becomes filled to the brim but the sensations continue to stimulate, it releases its pressure through vomiting.

Sadness. When the sadness container can no longer contain the stimulation it is receiving, tears automatically begin to flow.

Joy. When the container of joy is overstimulated, you start laughing.

Aversion. The overfilling of this container makes you shake your head and whine.

Fear. When pressure builds up inside this container, it is released through screaming.

Anger. A full-blown anger episode causes rapid breathing, redness of the face, restlessness, yelling, and swearing—all of which reduce the pressure in the container. If they do not, then anger can go upward along your back and neck, making you develop a headache.

Anxiety. When anxiety gets too intense, the sensation of its container completely disappears, and you hands and your voice begin to tremble, your appetite may disappear or become greater (that depends on other factors), and you may get the sensation of something stuck in your throat.

Sexual Desire. When this area becomes overstimulated, the natural output is orgasm, but that does not usually happen automatically. This is because this area is not a container, and it does not have boundaries, which channel emotion. The sex-drive area cannot get enough stimulation. To "spill," it usually requires help from an external source, if you know what I mean.

## Summary

All emotions that you can possibly experience, you always experience in your torso. Not only do feelings never appear in your arms, legs, or head, but they only appear in specific, designated areas of your torso, which never change. Sadness always feels like heaviness in the sides of your chest. Aversion encloses the center of your chest, where joy is located. The sides of your upper abdomen contain anger, while anxiety occupies your solar plexus. Disgust lies in the middle of your abdomen, and below its container is the area of sexual desire. The only emotion that you experience in your back is fear—deep in the ribcage, between the lower edges of the shoulder blades and the waist. Behind and between the areas that contain fear is the area in which the push that always accompanies daydreams and that reinforces every feeling originates.

Over all, there are eight emotion-producing areas, five singles and three doubles: one for disgust, one for aversion, one for joy, one for anxiety, one for sexual desire, and two each for sadness, anger, and fear. All of these areas with the exception of the one for sexual desire "contain" their designated feelings, and therefore we will be calling them *containers* throughout this book.

The container of joy begins filling from its lowest point, which is right above the depth of the solar plexus and moves upward whenever the emotion of joy becomes stronger. The container of aversion also starts filling up from the bottom, spiraling upward around the container of joy. The containers of sadness become active starting from the bottom and moving upward, but the containers of anger start filling with the emotion from two spots near the surface of your body and then spread into its depth. The container of anxiety becomes active deep in the solar plexus, spreading the sensations that indicate anxiety to your mind forward to the abdomen's surface. The containers of fear become active beginning with the points in the depths, then spread from those inner regions backward, carrying the sensation of fear to the back's surface. The container of disgust, too, fills up from its deepest and lowest point, spreading upward only when the feeling has occupied the container widthwise. The area of sex drive occupies the whole lower abdomen below the container of disgust, and, similarly to anger, begins its activation at two small areas near the surface of the lower abdomen. This area does not really contain any feelings per se but resets your body and mind to the sexual mode.

When the container of joy fills up to the brim, it releases the pressure via laughter. Excessive sadness is released through tears. When anxiety becomes too intense, it makes your hands and voice tremble—unlike anger, which makes you breathe rapidly and causes you to become red in the face and restless and to start yelling and swearing. Strong disgust manifests itself through vomiting, and powerful aversion causes you to shake your head and whine. The container of fear decompresses by means of screaming, and, finally, when the area of sexual desire becomes overactive—which means that your entire mindset has switched to the sex-driven mode—it will push you to take action. If no other feeling in this mode stands in its way, then all of your actions will lead you toward the goal of having sex.

# CHAPTER 2: EMOTIONS AND THE ACTIVATING BREATH

A few years ago, my friends Angela and Peter invited me to a birthday party for Peter, which they were having at their house. At the time, their son, Justin, was four years old. Most of the gifts that the guests brought were intended, of course, for Peter, but some guests also brought something for the little boy. One of these gifts was a box of crayons, which somebody handed Justin without letting his parents know. (I said it then and I say it now: I did not give the crayons to the little vandal! My gift was a set of toy soldiers.) Well, when Justin's mother walked into the living room and saw that the wall, which had been recently painted, had been thoroughly colored with Justin's drawings, the sound of her gasp—followed by a series of emotionally charged exclamations—traveled to the farthest corners in the house. That loud gasp marked a change in Angela's feelings. It was so loud because of the great difference in intensity between Angela's emotion *before* the moment when she saw the expression of her son's creativity on the wall and the emotions she felt as she made the discovery.

Breathing is inseparable from emotions. A mere instant before you experience a feeling, your breathing changes in intensity and depth (or location). As you learned in the last chapter, each emotion has its own location in the body, which never changes.

We intuitively understand the connection between breathing and emotion. For example, picture a man whose face is red, whose nostrils are flared, and who is breathing forcefully and rapidly. You immediately recognize that this man is angry. From your experience, you know that this is not the way anyone breathes normally, and therefore you can safely assume that this man does not breathe this way all the time. There must have been a certain point at which his emotion and his breathing changed from some other feeling to anger.

But the connection between breathing and emotion is not always obvious. For instance, if you observe someone who is worried, you won't see flared nostrils or rapid breathing. You might have to listen very carefully to hear how the person's voice sounds weaker than usual or is actually trembling. And of course people frequently keep their emotions to themselves, bottled up. But all this does not mean that their breathing does not change. There is simply no way for emotions to change without breathing's involvement.

The fact that switching from one feeling to another is always accompanied by a change in breathing means that breath can be used to control emotion. This chapter focuses on the use of breathing to interrupt this "natural" transition from one emotional state to another. But first, let's look at another tool in your toolbox—one that can help you closely observe yourself. As you'll find, observing yourself will equip you with practical knowledge about controlling your emotions.

## Bodily Imagination

This powerful tool is your *imagination*. Imagination is indispensable for learning to control your emotions, and, as with any other tool, your proficiency in using it will grow with practice.

Imagination gives you amazing freedom: to remember the past and construct the future, to fly high in the sky and dive deep to the bottom of the ocean, to bring yourself pleasure or to do things that are harmful to your body. But imagination is not just a mental phenomenon. Your ability to imagine depends upon the experiences you've had during your life, but your memory of those experiences isn't stored only in your mind. Just as you feel emotions in your body, your memories of emotional experiences are stored in your body.

The mind and the body remember things differently, and mental memory can sometimes be highly "edited." For example, if you *think* about the trip that you took a couple of years ago, you might choose to remember the good weather you enjoyed and the breathtaking architecture you saw. But if you tap into the memory of that trip that is stored in your body, you might remember feeling lost in an unfamiliar city, feeling confused because you did not know the language, feeling hungry, worrying about not being able to find a bathroom quickly enough, or being sickened by that persistent, gut-wrenching cocktail of smells—from disinfectant to cigarettes—that seemed embedded into the very walls and floor of your hotel room!

You should have no problem remembering those kinds of details about various events if you truly try to recall them viscerally. When you really can't, then remember anything that happened before or after the event that you are trying to recall, focusing your attention on details. If there's a real connection to the event you're trying to remember, you'll be led to those visceral memories you're trying to recall.

Doing this, however, requires concentration. What is concentration? Imagine you are in the seventh grade, and your math teacher has just asked you a question. You think you know the answer, and yet you cannot quite remember it. You feel uncomfortable: your classmates are staring at you; you're tired because you stayed up too late the night before; you did not do the homework for the next class; and you cannot afford another F—not to mention another talk with your parents! Your teacher tells you, "Concentrate," but that's not very helpful.

When you are living through a number of experiences simultaneously, they're all competing for your attention. Some of these experiences may be thoughts, but not all of them—and, in fact, thoughts may have a pretty low priority. If you were that seventh-grader, which of the following experiences would occupy your attention more: trying to remember the answer to the question that your teacher has asked you or facing another talk with your parents about your falling behind in school? And having stayed up too late does not help, either. The desire to sleep consumes much more of your attention than trying to find the answer to an abstract question that is irrelevant to you on the emotional level. All these emotions fight very effectively for your attention, and when you need to concentrate—which basically means to turn your attention to a specific subject—you simply do not have enough power to free your mind from the tenacious grasp of your feelings.

Being asked to concentrate can, in other words, put you in a vicious circle, one that you may encounter when trying to perform the exercises in this book. To learn to control your emotions, you'll need your concentration to guide your imagination, and yet, if you do not know how to control your emotions, your focus will stay dispersed. But do not panic. Throughout this book, I will be asking you to do many different stunts in your imagination. To do them well, all you need is to stay calm and motionless *to the best of your ability*—just as you do when you daydream. And after you do a few of the exercises described here, you'll begin to be able to manipulate your concentration even when you are preoccupied by thoughts or feelings.

## The Activating Inhalation

Imagine yourself at work. You are doing your regular job, which you know how to do very well because you have been doing it for years, when your boss comes over and begins telling you that you are doing it all wrong. You want to avoid a conflict and so you suppress your urge to tell him what you really think—that he's incompetent and stupid, that his mother must have been drunk while she was pregnant with him, that his wife is undoubtedly unfaithful, and that his dog has a questionable pedigree. Instead, you compose yourself and handle the critique in your usual easy-going way.

Your ability to control yourself in this manner is a truly amazing acquired skill. It has taken you years of hard work to learn to behave in certain ways in situations like this. You've already got the technique; you've just got to learn how to recognize it and summon it for use in modifying any feeling that you believe needs alteration. So let us look carefully at what you did when your boss criticized you and at how, exactly, you subdued your emotions in that interaction.

When your boss began criticizing your work, your mind interpreted what he said as an attack. Clearly, this attack was not life-threatening, which why your immediate reaction was not to run away but rather to fight back—hopefully by means of words and not fists. But this is where your self-control intervened. To curb your response, you momentarily stopped breathing. What is especially important is that *you instinctively stopped breathing during the very inhalation that switched your emotional state.* What you did was deprive the feeling's container of something that is essential to the feeling's formation.

This "essential something" is *not* air. Think about it: The leading emotion in this particular blend of feelings would most likely be anger, and anger's container is located in the upper abdomen. You could not possibly be depriving that area of air, simply because air does not go any farther down into your body than your lungs. (If it does, then controlling your emotions is probably the least of your problems, and you need to consult a doctor immediately!) If you closely observe what you instinctively did, you'll see that all you did was to stop the *movement* of breathing in the area of the emotion's container.

Now, let's look at the first technique for interrupting a feeling's formation.

Once the inhalation stops, the anger formation stops with it—making it clear that the inhalation process is a major component of feeling generation. You then draw another breath, which you innately aim at the place in your body where the leading emotion of your new emotional blend takes shape, the one that is behind your good-natured response. In other words, you *redirect* the inhalation toward a different emotional container. As you think about this, it's important to remember that only inhalations—never exhalations—can activate feelings.

**Exercise: Introduction to Intervening in Activating Inhalation**

Before we get to the actual exercise, let me say a few words about what you need to keep in mind while doing any of the exercises described in this book. The purpose of all the exercises is to develop the skills necessary to apply the techniques that the book explains. Because you probably want to be able to use these techniques in your life, it is best to do the exercises in states close to your real, waking life. For instance, it is very unusual to keep your eyes closed in real-life situations, which means that you should not close your eyes while you are doing the exercises. Since the situations that trigger unwanted emotions in you mostly occur while you are sitting or standing, then these are the positions in which you should do your exercises. You might experience difficulty using some techniques, and to get a better grasp on the sensations that a feeling consists of, you may want to lie down for the exercise. When you begin to get results, however, change your body's posture to the one in which this troublesome emotion normally occurs.

When you practice, try not to shift your eyes. Pick some point in your view and focus your eyes on it. When your eyes move, they can distract you from your exercise. Once you know how to apply the technique you have worked on, you will need to keep your eyes still for only an instant when using the technique in your day-to-day life.

A crucial point to remember is to keep your torso still and avoid slouching during the exercises. To learn to control your emotions, you need to identify and memorize the sensations that occur in the feelings' containers while you are experiencing the emotions that are the focus of your exercise. Your ability to observe the emotions' containers while the feelings appear and disappear in them is what allows you to collect the information on how those emotions occur as well as how your body and mind naturally turn your feelings on and off.

For your first exercise, remember a situation from your own life in which you became very angry at someone. Again, try to remember it not just in your mind but also in your body. Try to *relive* the moment in your imagination and in your breathing. And as you do so, look for that first inhalation that activates your anger.

Now, replay the scenario, but stop breathing right when that anger-activating inhalation is about to start. Do you suddenly feel as if you were suffocating? You may, despite the fact that your breathing has been interrupted for only a fraction of a second. This feeling of suffocation shows you the intensity of the emotion that is about to appear and also the intensity of the inhalation that it takes to activate this emotion.

Now imagine the same situation again, but this time, instead of holding your breath, inhale more than you need; make sure that you do so *exactly* during the inhalation that triggers your anger. Try not to overdo it, though. Judging by the intensity of the feeling of suffocation that you felt when you stopped breathing, you should be able to predict how much more you need to inhale. If you do it right, your anger will immediately become significantly weaker, as if has been watered down.

As I already mentioned, the actual drawing in of air is unimportant in this metamorphosis. What's essential is the breathing process itself, which is a series of very specific movements.

Now, let's begin developing greater control in directing your breathing toward the locations where emotions form. To do that, we'll need to consider in detail three different levels of breathing: breathing with the chest, breathing with the upper abdomen, and breathing with the lower abdomen.

## Breathing with Your Chest

Let us start with the most common and easiest level—breathing with your chest. Usually, when people breathe with their chests, their chests expand forward. But to use chest-level breathing to control emotion, you'll have to alter that process somewhat.

Sadness is one of the emotions whose container is located in the chest. To recall how sadness feels, try imagining the following situation: You have been working at a nursing home for several years. When you first took the job, you were able to shake off the depressing effects of having to deal, daily, with elderly people's suffering—their constant aches, their difficulty walking, their dementia, their unhappiness. But as time has passed, their suffering has become more painful to you, and it has made you sharply aware of your own mortality. Now, the thought that you, too, are going to grow old and become unable to take care after yourself is always at the forefront of your mind. You keep thinking about how your own children will someday send you to a nursing home just like the one where you work. Your sadness is taking over, dragging you down, making it harder and harder to do your job. Do you feel where the sadness is located in your body?

**Exercise: Intervening in Sadness Formation**

Now, think of a situation that has made you intensely sad. Observe where the container for this feeling is located. It's in the chest, yes, but the container of sadness extends outward to the shoulders. Assume the same body posture in which this feeling has bothered you most often in the past. If you experience difficulty doing this exercise in that position, you can change your pose in any way that makes it easier for you to identify the sensations that comprise sadness, but as soon as you've identified those sensations, change the pose back to the one in which you had trouble with this emotion originally and repeat the exercise in that pose.

As you relive the sadness in your imagination, try to catch the inhalation that activates your sad mode. At the instant of that inhalation, inhale more than you need to. The sadness you feel at the center of your chest becomes weaker, but the regions of the container that are closer to the shoulders remain unaffected, still holding your sadness. To eliminate the feeling entirely, you are going to need to reach all the corners of the container. And to do that, you will have to expand your chest sideways—rather than forward—during the inhalation.

To give yourself better control over this "sideways" breathing, raise your hands and press your palms against each other in front of your chest, thus decreasing the weight of your arms on your shoulders and reducing the pressure on the sides of your chest. (Ordinarily, it's the weight of your arms that causes you to expand your chest forward rather than to the sides when you breathe.) If you are sitting in a chair with arms, then you can place your arms on the arms of the chair—pay particular attention that your elbows are resting comfortably on the chair's arms—and this will also reduce your arms' weight on your shoulders and chest. Now, again try to catch the inhalation that activates your sadness, and again inhale more than you need—but this time let your chest expand to the sides. Your inhalation will fill the entire container of sadness, making you feel that you've diluted your sadness with just one breath.

**Exercise: Intervening in Aversion Formation**

Imagine that it's Friday afternoon at your workplace. You are looking forward to the coming weekend, when your boss tells you that the firm is failing to meet a deadline and that she really needs you to work the next day. Obviously, you do not want to work on the weekend, but how do you know that? What is the feeling that you're experiencing? And more important, where is it located? Let us call this feeling *aversion*, and you should feel it near the middle of your chest. As happens with all emotions, your aversion is activated by one single inhalation, which you need to catch.

Now, imagine this situation one more time, focusing on the emotional transformation that occurs at the moment you hear that half your weekend is being canceled, and inhale more than you feel the urge to during the very inhalation that makes the switch. Your aversion should not form, and you are probably surprised that the prospect of working on Saturday does not affect your mood! But notice that you've managed to stop aversion's formation using your normal breathing with your chest. It means that in this case, your natural breathing with your chest, during which your chest expands forward, does the job well and does not require modification (as it did when you were intervening in sadness's formation).

Next, think of any situation from your past in which you experienced aversion, and inhale more than you feel the urge to with the inhalation that turns on your aversion. If you do it well, you should remember the situation clearly—but the aversion that is part of your emotional response to that situation should not appear. Repeat this exercise with several more aversion-provoking situations from your past, until you feel comfortable intervening in aversion's activation whenever you wish to disrupt it.

## Breathing with Your Upper Abdomen

There are two ways to breathe with your upper abdomen. With the first technique, you'll be able to influence the appearance of emotions whose containers are located nearer the surface of your body. With the second, you'll control emotions that are located deeper within the body.

In the first method, the inhalation takes some effort: you inhale by deliberately expanding your ribcage. During the exhalation, however, you simply relax; your ribcage pushes the air out of your lungs as the result of your upper abdomen returning to its initial position. In the second method, you constrict your muscles during *exhalation,* making your ribcage move inward and squeezing the air out of your lungs. In this method, it's the inhalation that takes place automatically when you relax your muscles and allow your upper abdomen to return to its normal shape.

Let's look at specific applications of these two techniques:

**Exercise: Intervening in Anger Formation**

As we've already discussed, pockets of anger can expand deep into your body. But anger, like any emotion, has a starting point or points—epicenters in your body where the feeling ignites. Anger's two ignition points are located near the surface of your body, approximately where the front and the sides of your ribcage meet. Intense anger spreads deeper into the ribcage, creating a sensation of your body splitting into upper and lower halves along the connection line between the ignition points. But you want to stop this emotion—before it becomes uncontrollable rage!—by influencing the *first* breath that activates it. Therefore, your attention should focus on the superficial ignition points. If you intervene at the instant of the initial inhalation, your anger will not progress any further.

We've all been in situations that have inflamed our anger. Imagine, for example, that you're living in an apartment right below an elderly but *unbelievably* agile couple. This old couple wakes up very early every morning and immediately starts making a lot of noise. You hear metal pans being dropped on the tile floor, furniture being dragged around the apartment, and footsteps that sound as if a herd of horses were being chased by a large predator that has hooves instead of paws! You used to go upstairs every couple of days and politely ask the couple to try to be a little bit quieter. They always assured you that from that point on you would not hear a peep out of them—but every morning the story repeats itself. Imagine yourself lying in bed, listening to the chairs scraping the floor above and wondering how soon you'll be able to move to another apartment. Meanwhile, your thoughts about the elderly couple are turning murderous. You may not ever have been in exactly this situation, but I'm sure you can identify.

Now, recall a situation from your own life that provoked your anger. Imaginatively relive that situation, concentrating on your bodily memory of the event. Do it while either sitting or standing, but because you'll have to reach closer to the surface of your upper abdomen with your breathing, keep the front of your torso relaxed, motionless, and slightly arched forward. As your anger is about to start, catch the initial, activating inhalation, and inhale more deeply than you feel you have the need to, using the first breathing method, in which you put your effort into expanding your ribcage during inhalation.

As you do this exercise, you may notice that your mind is treating your breathing as a separate event from your emotional reaction, causing you to focus on the breathing rather than the emotion. But this is counterproductive, because you need to concentrate on the emotion's formation, imaginatively reliving the situation from your past as if it were happening now. To prevent your mind from being distracted in this way, try to apply only minimal effort, focusing more on the precision of your breathing, so that your intentional drawing in additional breath will smoothly blend with the activating inhalation that turns on your anger, giving it a boost to expand past its preset boundaries. To do that, you need to move the starting point of your breathing closer to anger's ignition points. As you try this, you will see that when you breathe with your upper abdomen, you can shift the place from which you start expanding your abdomen higher or lower, deeper or closer to the surface. The closer your starting point is to the ignition points, the more immediately and completely your anger will disappear. You will know that you've done this exercise correctly when your anger immediately turns into a sensation resembling that of two small, inflated balloons, one inside each of anger's two ignition points.

**Exercise: Intervening in Anxiety Formation**

Although anxiety's container is also located in the upper abdomen, it is much deeper inside the body than that of anger. To reach the anxiety container, you must therefore employ a different breathing technique.

You feel worry in the middle of your solar plexus and about a hand's width to the right and left, behind the ribcage. Anxiety has only one ignition point—deep within the solar plexus, near or on the abdominal midline. The breathing technique you used to dilute anger cannot reach anxiety's pocket, so you'll need to employ a technique that takes your breathing deeper.

I'm sure you've experienced strong worry or anxiety at some time in your life. Here's an example of a situation that would provoke overwhelming anxiety: Imagine that you are a professional masseur and have incorporated your business. All of the sudden, you receive a letter from the IRS saying that your company is going to be audited. Your accountant has promised to prepare all the required paperwork. She has also told you that she saw three audits of this sort last year and that there is no need for you to worry. But you cannot help it; you worry.

Interestingly, anxiety often compels you to look for an explanation of the situation that you find yourself in—as if discovering some logic behind the events would make you feel a little bit better. But if you tackle the emotion itself, you won't need to rationalize something that may, in fact, make no sense and over which you have no control. To stop anxiety, you'll use the following breathing method:

When exhaling, draw your upper abdomen inward, squeezing the air out of your lungs. Then, to inhale, slowly relax your upper abdomen; as it returns to its initial form, your abdomen will cause your lungs fill up with air. (If you feel that you are not inhaling enough air, it means that your chest is becoming involved in your breathing. To keep the chest out of it, relax your chest and do not let it move while you are breathing.)

As we already discussed in the previous technique, just as every feeling has an ignition point, so does every inhalation or exhalation's movement have a starting point—the place at which inhalation or exhalation begins. Your effortful exhalation, in this case, can start near the surface of your upper abdomen or deep inside the solar plexus. With some practice, you can also shift the starting point farther up, down, or to the sides. The same is true with the inhalation. But do not get confused: Although we are discussing both inhalation and exhalation here, we are only talking about the breathing technique. The application of this technique remains the same throughout this chapter—to intervene in the activating *inhalation*.

Although inhalation, in this case, does not require effort and occurs automatically, its movement is tied up with the starting point of your exhalation. So, for better results, you should try to move the exhalation's starting point as close as you can to the anxiety's ignition point deep in your solar plexus, so that the feeling will not even begin to form. You will not be able to make the exhalation's starting point precisely touch anxiety's ignition point, unfortunately, but try to do your best. Because there is no way to *exactly* superimpose the starting point of inhalation on anxiety's ignition point, the inhale-more-than-you-need technique does not destroy anxiety completely, leaving a little bit of it deep under your chest. That little bit that is left, however, should not bother you all that much.

Now, recall a situation that has made you feel anxious, reliving it in your imagination. During the breath that activates the anxiety, inhale more than you feel the urge to. At this point, you should not feel worried. There is a little side effect in this case. Because the starting point of your breath and anxiety's ignition point cannot be superimposed, as you inhale more than you need to, you will, for a brief moment, feel as if your anxiety is about to appear. It does, in fact, appear, but only in that small area between the starting and ignition points. Anxiety, then, almost immediately disappears. It turns into the same sensation of a balloon that you felt when you turned off your anger, but in this case the sensation of a balloon appears in your solar plexus, deeper in your body than you felt it with the diluted anger. Also, this sensation of a balloon is much milder for modified anxiety then it is for anger. When you inhale more than you need, you plug that sensation of the hole, so to speak, creating the sensation that feels only a little bit more pronounced than that of the active anxiety container.

**Exercise: Intervening in Fear Formation**

Intervening in fear formation also requires the forceful exhalation technique. Similarly to anxiety, fear becomes active deep inside your upper abdomen, but then it spreads toward your back, filling the containers of fear. The activating inhalation is therefore directed toward your back. Just imagine yourself sitting by a window, sipping coffee, enjoying the quiet evening, when suddenly you hear a loud explosion. In this sort of situation, you often hear people gasp. That gasp is the activating breath that turns on fear. For a brief moment, when your fear is about to start, you can feel an urge to inhale more than you did during the preceding breaths. If, however, you draw in *even more air* than you feel like inhaling right before your fear is about to appear, then your fright will either become weaker or will not appear at all.

To stop fear from appearing at all, your intentional exaggeration of the activating inhalation needs to go completely beyond the container's boundaries. You can feel these boundaries clearly an instant before the activating inhalation takes place. In fact, this clear outline of the container is what focuses your breathing on the container of fear (although the same is true with all other feelings) and triggers the urge in you to inhale more. But note that the urge to inhale does not simply mean to inhale more, but, rather, to inhale *a very specific amount of air*. This is why even a clumsy attempt to inhale more damages the feeling, and inhaling much more—so that your body and mind no longer recognize the activating breath of the preset emotion—resets your emotional state.

## Breathing with Your Lower Abdomen

Breathing with your lower abdomen is done the same way as the deep breathing with your upper abdomen. You force the air out of your lungs by drawing your lower abdomen, which is the part below your navel, inward. When you release your lower abdomen, it returns to its initial shape, while drawing air into your lungs.

Beginners frequently experience two difficulties with this breathing technique. The first one is chest interference—which, again, you can solve by keeping your chest relaxed and not allowing it to start moving. The second difficulty is not being able to make the breathing reach the lower abdomen—that is, having the sensation that the inhalation is getting stuck just below the chest. If you have this difficulty, the problem is probably in your posture. You can solve the problem by relaxing your hip and pelvic muscles and letting your pelvis drop and sway a little bit forward, thus creating the effect of your upper body pressing down on your lower abdomen. Try to achieve an equal sense of relaxation in your body either standing up or sitting down or even lying down—whichever position you feel most comfortable in. When you get results in the position that you find most comfortable—say, lying on your back—try to achieve the same results in the other positions, such as standing or sitting. If this does not solve your problem, then pay attention to the areas of your torso in which you feel discomfort. Whether it is your chest or upper abdomen, try to relax it. If your breathing still does not reach your lower abdomen, try breathing with the lower abdomen more forcefully.

By breathing with lower abdomen, you can destroy the emotions that you experience in that area, such as sexual desire. You can also prevent the feeling of disgust from appearing, despite its container being located in the middle of your abdomen. The reason why you affect disgust with the lower rather than with the upper abdomen is that you redirect the formation of emotions from one pocket to another by tensing up the region of the abdominal muscles that is located *below* the container to which you redirect your mind's attention.

**Exercise: Intervening in Disgust Formation**

Suppose you've found a dead coyote in your backyard. Say your first instinct is to quietly relocate the carcass onto your neighbor's property. That task, however, proves to be more difficult than you thought. As you pull on the dead animal's hind legs, its internal organs fall out, and the pungent stench of the rotting flesh hits your nose like an explosion, immediately reaching deep into your guts and making them rumble. Observe carefully: the ignition point of disgust is located deep inside the abdomen, slightly above the navel. Activation of this point occurs when your lower abdomen contracts and reaches an intensity that triggers your disgust and then, if the intensity of the feeling increases further, makes you vomit. Note that the abdominal contraction is greater *below* the actual container of the feeling. To fully stop the formation of disgust, you can use the inhale-more-than-you-need technique, but you need to do it with your lower and upper abdomen simultaneously. And as you include your upper abdomen in your inhalation, you have to employ the deep breathing technique—that is, the technique with the forceful exhalation—for that area.

Now, think of the gross coyote carcass again, and at the same time begin exhaling simultaneously with your upper and lower abdomen, but make sure that the movement of your exhalation starts deep inside your belly, as close as possible to disgust's ignition point. Almost immediately, you will feel a forceful but focused inhalation that turns on the container of disgust, if you have not lost the mental image of the smelly carcass. Inhale more than you feel the urge to with that activating breath. Your feeling of disgust will not be formed, and the movement of that excessive inhalation will disperse through the abdomen.

Try to recall any situation from your past in which you experienced disgust. Whatever the situation was, observe carefully which sensations mean disgust for you. Now try to follow those sensations with your breathing. As you did before, make sure that you inhale more than you feel the urge to and channel that inhalation right where you experience those sensations. If the sensations of your inhalation reach the sensations that mean disgust to you, your disgust will not appear.

**Exercise: Intervening in Activation of Sexual Desire**

Suppose you are busy with important work, which requires your full concentration, and persistent erotic thoughts keep popping into your mind. You can feel that the area of your sexual drive is active, and you decide to tone it down, so you can go back to work. But, since you missed the activating inhalation that turned on your sex drive, you summon another mental picture that you find even more sexually exciting and inhale more than you need with the new activating inhalation, using the your lower abdomen. But you feel that it is making matters worse!

Remember that the area of sexual desire is not a container: it does not contain your libido; what it does is to switch your sexual excitement on and off, resetting your entire mindset to the sex-driven mode. When you inhale more than you feel the urge to with your lower abdomen, you will only increase your excitement. To tone it down, on the other hand, your efforts should be much more intuitive: Simply do not let yourself draw the air in deeper during activating inhalation—particularly, do not let your breathing reach to your lower abdomen—and you can stay focused on the work that you are doing. You will not feel that you are suffocating—as you would if you did this to any of the other emotions' containers. Your sexual drive will switch off after just a few breaths if you do not give it the necessary energy, which comes from the inhalation.

## The Relative Intensity of Emotions

Suppose that many of your coworkers have been laid off, and you are worried that you may be next in line for a pink slip. At lunchtime, you take a walk down the street. You're aware of your surroundings—you notice that it's warm and sunny; you hear the sound of cars driving by; and your eye is momentarily caught by a funny-looking dog who's trotting by, sniffing the ground—but none of these things really distracts you from your worries. Then, all of a sudden, you notice a hundred-dollar bill lying on the pavement. No one seems to be looking, and you quickly squat down and pick up that hundred with one swift movement of your hand, barely interrupting your pace. For the next few minutes, you are smiling, savoring your catch. And for the next ten minutes, you stop worrying about losing your job. Yes, you have definitely become a hundred dollars richer, and yes, you may keep the money, but the really interesting thing is that you have managed, somehow, to *turn off* your previous emotion. Let's take a look at how you accomplished that.

You already know where and how you feel worry. But let us see out how one situation can distract you from whatever you're experiencing at a given moment, while another situation does not have that power. Recall that, in the scenario above, you did notice the weather, the cars, and the dog—meaning that each of these things made you experience certain emotions, though none was powerful enough to distract you. But when you saw the money, the emotion you experienced at that moment took over your attention. And just as the emotion that was activated when you saw the hundred-dollar bill had great intensity, so did the inhalation of breath that activated it.

As you are walking down the street weighing your fears about losing your job, you are experiencing a fairly complex *blended* emotion, which means that you feel several areas of your body more clearly than you usually do. These sensations are similar to the feeling of mild discomfort. (The precise mix of emotions would depend on what keeping your job means to you.) How clearly, or pronouncedly, you feel each of the emotions in the blend is what we call the emotion's *intensity*. When you notice the weather, the cars, and the dog, you feel places other than the worry container "turning on" in your torso. From moment to moment, your emotional pattern is subtly rearranged, but none of these feelings has a great enough intensity to displace your leading emotion: worry.

And then you see the hundred-dollar bill, and your entire emotional pattern changes. What is so special about this change is that the new feeling's intensity has moved past a certain threshold, redirecting your attention away from your worry over losing your job and to the sudden, confident feeling that accompanies finding money.

Let's try to find the activating inhalation that made that emotional switch possible. Most likely, you would feel the anxiety over possibly losing your job as a trembling located deep in your solar plexus, extending approximately a hand's width to the right and left under your ribcage. As soon as you notice the hundred-dollar bill, this trembling becomes weaker. To understand this effect, ask yourself what money means to you—not philosophically but *emotionally*. To do that, picture yourself having more money—I mean *a lot* more. Imagine that you have several houses, a few businesses that provide well for you, and more money in the bank than you could spend in a lifetime. What do you feel? Do you feel how the same place in your body in which you experience worry becomes more stable? Do you feel, as you imagine yourself being very rich, how you draw a much deeper breath that goes straight to your solar plexus? This happens because money gives you confidence, and this emotion activates the same container as that of anxiety. Confidence, however, does not have a dedicated container. It appears automatically when your anxiety diminishes. In other words, you experience perfect self-confidence when your anxiety is completely gone.

Now, suppose your wealthy uncle—whom you did not even know existed!—all of a sudden gives you two thousand dollars. How does this amount make you feel? Is the inhalation that forms your emotional response different? Has the trembling diminished much? What if your newly discovered uncle were to give you five thousand dollars? Twenty thousand? Let's make it an even billion and leave it at that. By comparing how increasing amounts of money affect your emotional pattern and—more important to this exercise—how each affects your breathing, you can see that your feeling of worry or confidence is connected to the degree of trembling that you experience deep in your upper abdomen and the way you draw your breaths differently every time the degree of trembling changes.

Now I want you to pay close attention to the changes that occur in your breathing. Every time you imagine a greater amount of money and your emotional state changes, your breathing becomes more focused and more forceful, but not necessarily deeper. Rather, you recognize in these sums (as you did in that hundred-dollar bill) something that you wished for, or, rather, an opportunity to cancel your worries. That recognition opens up something in you that allows you to shift your emotions. The point is that whatever that something is, it does not come into your body from the outside and seems to be under the full control of your mind. But there is a problem: The new emotional pattern that comes from your finding the hundred-dollar bill doesn't have enough power to sustain your good mood; once you go back to work or even just begin thinking about the layoffs again, your mood will change back to being worried.

But how did this switch occur? Partly, it's a matter of perspective. A large bus looks small when seen from a distance; likewise, when you were out walking, the problems at work seemed smaller and more distant than that hundred-dollar bill lying right in front of you. When you go back to work, however, your job-related problems again become bigger, like an approaching bus. This problem of situations getting progressively worse in your mind needs to be addressed. Let us call these strings of related situations *cascading*.

## Cascading Situations

We've looked at a few ways to use breathing to intervene in the formation of emotion. But there's a problem with these techniques as explained so far: They're situational. The application of the breathing technique works once—but when another situation arises, you'll have to use it again. For example, if you use an exaggerated inhalation to stop the formation of the anxiety that appears in response to one of your coworkers being laid off, you will have to use it again if another coworker gets the boot, because your feeling will most likely come back. And your worry will definitely come back if your own employment with the company comes into question—for example, if you receive an unexpected email from your boss saying that she wants to speak with you. You can use the technique of interfering with the emotion's activating breath every time there is a change in the situation—and, indeed, this can be a solution—but there is another approach, which would cover the numerous twists that might occur in a situation over time.

Think of what it is, exactly, that keeps you at work. (By "think," I mean *observe what you feel in your torso*.) For most people, the most important reason to work may be to earn money—to have a steady flow of income that considerably exceeds the one-time benefit of a hundred dollars found in the street.

How can you know that *your* reason for coming to work is to earn money? To figure it out, use your imagination. Imagine that you have more money than you could possibly spend in a lifetime and that there is no way you can lose that money. (In your imagination, this can easily be true.) Would you still want to work at the same place? But don't "think" about it; instead, observe what your visceral response is—the response of your emotional containers. If your imagination tells you that you would lose interest in your work, it means that you work for money. Now that you know this, you can intentionally take your anxiety to a deeper level. To do this, allow your imagination to develop a worst-case scenario: you lose your job, you can't find another, you have no money left, you have no place to live. You're spending every waking hour trying to find food. In other words, let your worry take control of your imagination. Go as far as you can with this in your imagination while still feeling that you can regain control, and then, when you feel that you are reaching the limit of how much of this horror you can take, stop this progression by inhaling more than you need. For better results, try to imagine such cascading situations very convincingly for yourself, but making them seem ultra real is not crucial to this technique. Your goal here still remains to identify and catch the activating breath, which is more difficult to identify in an imaginary situation, because the difference in the emotions' intensities is small and so is the difference in the inhalations that turn on these emotions.

If you closely observe what happens to your emotional state as you let your imagination picture the worst, you will see that it shifts very fast—much faster than it does in real life. These rapid changes, however, still occur with the help of your breathing: nearly every breath that you take while letting your worries take control over your mind activates a more intense level of anxiety and fear. At any moment, you can stop this terrifying progression of cascading images with an excessive inhalation and return your imagination to a comfortable state. By practicing this, you'll train yourself to allow your feelings take over your imagination and then to regain control. It will become second nature to you—like talking or walking. To a certain extent, this process is already part of your personality; the difference is that, as you live your life now, the surrounding environment has control over your emotions instead of you. But when you've practiced imagining a situation that you care about becoming emotionally intolerable, you are seizing your concentration, thus taking control over your emotions. Now, no matter what happens at your workplace, it will not stimulate your anxiety, because you know that you can stop it even at a much more intense stage. While you can disrupt or at least diminish the effect that unwanted feelings have on you even during your first attempts, usually it takes about two years of practice for two hours each day to develop a solid command of this technique.

## Summary

Emotions are inseparable from breathing. It is always an inhalation that switches on a feeling. In this book, we call this inhalation the *activating* inhalation. Because each emotion exists only in its designated container, the movement of the activating inhalation naturally reaches to every container in your body.

The main technique described in this chapter involves inhaling more than you feel the urge to during the activating inhalation, thus allowing you to disrupt the unwanted feeling's formation. The only exception is sexual desire, which requires a restricted inhalation. All containers of emotions are located in your torso, and you need to control your breathing well enough to intentionally reach every feeling's container in your body. To guide your breathing to the various containers, you need to employ one or more of the three levels of breathing: breathing with the chest, with the upper abdomen, and with the lower abdomen.

To fully access the emotions' containers in the chest, breathing can be done in two different ways: (1) the chest expands to the sides and (2) the chest expands forward. The containers of the upper abdomen are located either closer to the surface or deeper in the body and also requiring two different approaches: (1) the effort is applied during inhalation and (2) the effort is applied during exhalation. There is only one technique of breathing with the lower abdomen, in which only the exhalation requires an effort.

Whenever a feeling becomes active, its activation begins at one (if the emotion has only one container) or two (if the feeling has two symmetrical containers) *ignition* points. Similarly to feelings' activation, your breathing can also start from different points—farther up or down, right or left, deeper in your body or closer to the surface. To develop a faster and more effective control over the emotions' formation, you need to begin inhalation as close as you can to the feeling's ignition point. In those cases where exhalation requires an effort, you need to take into consideration that the inhalation that occurs automatically always returns to the points from which the exhalation started, which also needs to be near the emotion's ignition points. If you manage to bring the breath close enough to the ignition points, then the emotion will disappear instantly after its appearance.

To prepare yourself for dealing with stronger emotions, you can imagine increasingly more disturbing situations and exaggerate the activating inhalations that turn on your emotional reactions. Because the point of this exercise is to develop the skill of identifying and influencing the activating breath, you don't need to trick your mind into believing that you are actually living through the situations that you are imagining. All you need is to identify the activating breath. That, granted, is more difficult to do in an imaginary situation, but inhaling more than you feel the urge to during an activating inhalation that turns on an imaginary emotion will prepare you for dealing with a real-life situation, which has more to do with positioning the activating breath precisely than with the forcefulness of the breath.

# CHAPTER 3: EMOTIONS AND MOVEMENTS OF THE TORSO

Meet my friend George. George works in the customer service department of a small bank, and he hates his job. But despite the fact that the thought of going to work makes him feel mildly sick every morning, George manages to do his job exceptionally well. It takes a lot out of George to keep his current position, and he is always on a lookout for a more suitable place to work. I am rather embarrassed to admit, though, that I am glad that he finds himself doing work he hates, because if George loved his job, we wouldn't have the chance to study his remarkable talent for suppressing his true feelings.

If you compare how George stands, sits, and moves while he is at work with his body language during his off hours, you'll notice a great difference. At work, George moves a little bit slower, and although you can tell that he is not relaxed, his muscle tension never goes past a certain threshold. His posture is noticeably stooped forward, but he does not appear tired or sad; he seems, rather, alert. Finally, his speech is not as rushed and is much more carefully intonated than it is outside his workplace.

Whenever George is dealing with a disgruntled customer who makes him feel uncomfortable, he does not allow himself to fidget. With one decisive movement, he sways forward, placing his elbows on his desk, interlocking the fingers of his hands and leaning on his arms. These changes in George's behavior indicate that he uses shifts of his torso to control his emotions, which is the subject of this chapter. He naturally does a great job employing this method, but there is a still greater potential to this approach. In actuality, George could use the same techniques to turn off—rather than just repress—his annoyance with his job. He could, in fact, learn to regulate his emotions effortlessly.

Below, we look at three techniques for controlling feelings through shifts in the torso: (1) basic suppression, (2) forceful suppression, and (3) release of pressure. We're going to look at each of these techniques in relation to all eight of the "containers" discussed in earlier chapters. But before we do, I want you to note that there are problems with the way first two of these methods occur naturally.

While the first technique naturally represses emotions quickly and more or less effectively, it takes too much energy to keep your emotions bottled up—and when you have no energy to maintain the necessary degree of suppression, the repressed emotions can either seep through your self-control or even take complete control over your mind. And the second technique is even worse. The way it naturally occurs, it requires so much effort to repress the emotions and keep them repressed that they will almost inevitably reappear suddenly and forcefully. Observing these techniques when they occur naturally, however, can give you an indispensable insight in the nature of emotional control, and it can also give you a chance to figure out how you can tweak these instinctive techniques, so you can significantly increase their efficiency, as well as diminish their adverse effects.

Despite these techniques' negative side effects, however, we need to consider them very carefully, because they are the methods that our bodies and minds naturally and intuitively turn to every time we're in situations that require us to hide our true feelings. We therefore need to study them in depth before we can discuss the third method—a useful and effective technique that lets you *turn off* an emotion rather than repress it. Without first analyzing the ways our minds naturally use our bodies to suppress feelings, this third technique—which requires that you *not* repress your emotions—would be too difficult to explain. So let's begin.

## Technique 1: Basic Suppression

While it's true that this is the weakest and least effective technique for controlling emotion by shifting the torso, the fact that it is the most intuitive and most frequent naturally occurring approach to emotional control means that we need to take it into consideration. Here, we're going to lessen—or even eradicate—its adverse effects by observing, analyzing, and tweaking the mechanism. In many instances, the basic mechanism of this technique, led purely by the instinct—sometimes not just ineffectively but counterproductively—is almost the same for every feeling: whenever an emotion appears at a wrong time or place, you instinctively lean on the emotion's container with the weight of that part of the torso that's located above that container. A fundamental rule for lessening this technique's side effects is to press on the emotion's container during an early stage of feeling formation, thereby applying less effort to disrupt the emotion's appearance. Let's look at how that can be accomplished, beginning with the feeling of joy.

## Joy

Picture the following scenario: Rita is considering buying a house. Her real-estate agent shows her a house that is much bigger and better than she expected, and Rita really wants to buy it, but she needs to try to bargain the price down. So Rita suppresses her urge to jump for joy—because she does not want her agent to see her excitement—and acts as if she is hardly interested in this property. She feels the ticklish sensation of joy bubbling in the center of her chest, but she keeps the corners of her mouth and eyebrows turned down, slowly looking over the house as she might examine an old, worn-out, smelly pair of sneakers. When she asks the real-estate agent about the price, she firmly sets her mind to a haggling mode.

Imagine yourself in this or in a similar situation in which you've had to hide your excitement, and carefully observe how you suppress your joy. Because joy's container occupies the center of your chest, this area needs to be the focus of your attention. Notice how your excitement ignites from a single point at the bottom of the container of joy and then spreads upward along the midline of your chest in the direction of your head. As soon as you realize that you should not show your joy, you tilt your head and the part of your torso located right above the area of your chest into which your excitement has spread, blocking the further pathway of joy through its container. Your shoulders move slightly forward to add more firmness to your body's shift. Your excitement immediately stops forming and remains in the state that it had been in the moment you tilted your upper body forward.

**Exercise: Disruption of Joy**

Imagine yourself in the same situation several times in a row, and, each time, tilt your upper body in the same way that you naturally would to disrupt joy's formation. Do this at different stages of the feeling-forming process, noticing your instinctive interpretation of the sensations that mean joy to your mind. Notice, too, that this process starts with a smile and then develops into a full-fledged excitement, depending on how much of the container is being involved. By intervening at different stages, you can keep a greater or lesser degree of joy, depending on your goal, but you will never be able to deactivate the emotion completely this way. To turn off your joy entirely, you are going to need a slightly different approach.

Imagine the same situation again, but this time pay particularly close attention to the very beginning of your excitement. Try to identify your joy's ignition point—that is, the point from which your joy begins filling its container. Joy's single ignition point is located at the lowest point of the feeling's container. Upon close inspection, the very beginning of joy's formation feels like a miniature version of full-blown joy, but because it's concentrated in a very small area, you experience it as an intense "tickling." You need to memorize the sensation of your joy being triggered, because this sensation will give you the alarm whenever your excitement is about to go off in real life. There is also another reason for you to develop awareness of this sensation—so that you can remember the location of joy's ignition point. You can stop the development of your excitement at different stages by tilting your upper body forward at the right moment, but if you lean directly against the ignition point, the excitement will entirely disappear. What's more, you can extinguish your excitement by pressing on the ignition point *at any stage of the emotion's development.* Your joy will be totally gone.

**Aversion**

Sue is expected to go to a family reunion, but she really does not want to. On the one hand, she misses her relatives and does want to see them. But on the other, all the questions she anticipates being asked make her feel a bit sick: *You changed your job, again? When are you planning to get married? You look too skinny; don't you get enough to eat?* If she doesn't show up, however, she'll just be giving her relatives another reason to talk about her. She sighs deeply, noticeably slouches, and starts her preparation for the trip.

Picture yourself in a similar situation, or any other, in which you did not want to do something but had to suppress your reluctance and do it anyway. Observe how you naturally repress that reluctance. In this situation, your aversion is not too intense, as it does not fill its container entirely. That's because you do not find the feeling overwhelming or frightening, so it does not have the chance to manifest itself completely before you suppress it and act in spite of it. You sigh while pushing your whole chest a bit forward to mark the boundaries of the feeling's location within its container, and then you lean against it with the weight of your upper body, isolating your aversion from the rest of your emotional pattern. But notice that your reluctance does not disappear; it merely moves to the back of your mind and becomes only partly involved in your decision-making process. If you analyze these innate actions, however, you can gain much greater control over your aversion.

**Exercise: Disruption of Aversion**

Run through that same situation in your memory again, and carefully observe how your aversion starts and then spreads within its container. It ignites at two points located in the lower third of the container, behaving as if the feeling had two containers, one in each side of your chest. In fact, the sensation of twirling, which compels people to shake their heads, appears when aversion spreads from these two points, first in opposite directions but then sharply turning and circling around the container of joy and finally colliding at the back wall of the container, behind the container of joy.

Simply tilting your head and upper trunk forward will not be enough to disrupt aversion's formation, because there is not enough body weight to create the necessary pressure on the container of aversion. You also need to add pressure from the sides, so you can prevent the emotion from spreading toward the sides of your chest. This is accomplished by shifting your shoulders and the sides of your chest forward and down, thus firmly enwrapping the container of aversion. Make sure that you understand the mechanism by imagining the same situation again and observing how you do it instinctively. Now think about the same situation a few more times, performing the same shift of your body during different stages of the aversion's development. The form of the shift will remain nearly the same, but, each time, do it earlier and move it a tiny bit closer to the center of your chest. These manipulations will allow you to stop the progression of your aversion's development at different degrees, but they will not let you shut it down completely. To deactivate your reluctance fully, you again need to pay attention to the very beginning of the emotion's appearance.

The trick here—just as when you deactivated joy's formation—is to press on the ignition points. First, identify their location as precisely as you can, and then shift the sides of your chest and your upper torso so that you are pressing on the lower third of the container from both sides. Curiously, your shoulders will not move forward—as they normally do when repressing aversion—but, instead, they'll move backward and downward, enabling you to reach to the ignition points. Just as with the disruption of joy's formation, you can apply pressure directly to the ignition points at any stage of aversion's development to completely turn it off; the effect will be the same.

**Sadness**

Marsha's cat seemed not to be feeling well, so she decided to take it to the vet. She didn't think it was anything serious, so she was shocked when the vet told her that the cat was terminally ill and did not have much time to live. The vet recommended that Marsha leave her cat at the clinic, where the animal would be put to sleep. If she took her pet back home, the vet explained, the cat would soon be in excruciating pain and soon would die.

Marsha felt the tears rolling down her face. She had had this cat for more than ten years, and now, all of the sudden, she had to part with him. Stricken by grief, she left the cat at the vet's and went to work. Interestingly, she *was* able to do her work, even though her work required a lot of concentration. Yes, the cat was a very important part of her life, but she was able to suppress her grief and save it for later, when she returned home.

Perhaps you have also been able to effectively, if temporarily, suppress a feeling of sadness. Let's look at how the process works.

**Exercise: Disruption of Sadness**

Imagine yourself in a similar situation, and observe carefully how you can function when a strong emotion is being repressed. You may simply forget the feeling that you have repressed, or it may linger and consume part of your concentration. But let us analyze how the repression occurs, and then let's see if the feeling can, in fact, be forgotten.

When you imagine the loss of a beloved pet, you feel a heavy sensation filling the sides of your chest. You already know that this sensation indicates that your containers of sadness are being activated. Suppression of your sadness requires a sigh, which helps you to straighten your upper back and to pull your shoulders noticeably backward, thus allowing other emotions to run through your mind. This sigh and these small movements temporarily "quarantine" your grief, so to speak, letting you function despite being sad because your mind is only partly focused on your grief. (If the intensity of your sadness is too great, however, the sigh and the movement will not subdue the sensation, and you will not be able to focus on your work.)


Let us again look at how sadness becomes active. You can feel its ignition points, which are located on the sides of the containers that are closer to the chest's midline, in the upper third of the containers. The containers' activation begins at these ignition points and then spreads to the sides, filling the containers. When the containers are filled wall-to-wall from the bottom up, you feel the urge to slouch—and that, of course, is how you recognize when someone is feeling sad, because of his or her posture. Do notice that in the case of sadness, slouching does not disrupt the feeling. In fact, it makes it worse and keeps it stable. Keeping a straight posture, however, lets you suppress your sorrow. As with most other feelings, you need to press on the containers to prevent the emotion from gaining strength. Because slouching does not suppress sadness, however, you cannot use your upper body's weight to press on the containers. Instead, you use the weight of your arms together with that straight posture to suppress your grief either temporary or permanently.


Imagine yourself in a situation that has triggered your own sadness. Do this several times, and try suppressing the emotion at different stages of its development, moving progressively closer to sadness's ignition points. Notice that one of the most important things here is not to let your shoulders droop forward; instead, a gentle shift backward will give you access to the ignition points. Keeping pressure on the ignition points for a certain period—which may last from a few minutes to a few hours depending on the situation and on how strong your emotion is—will turn off the sadness permanently.

**Anxiety**

Natalie has a job interview in three minutes, and she is worried. She knows she has the right experience for the position and should feel confident, but she experiences anxiety before and during every job interview, like a nervous tic. But Natalie does not want the interviewer to see her nervousness, since that might ruin her chances of getting the job. So when the secretary invites her into a conference room, Natalie does her best to appear calm and smile, while stepping confidently through the open door.

Picture yourself in a situation in which you had to repress your anxiety. Most people naturally suppress their anxiety in the same way Natalie does: by pressing on the solar plexus—the place where we all feel anxiety—with the upper body. A problem with this method, however, is that after a minute or two, the trembling of your anxiety will start to seep through, and you'll start to feel worried again. When this happens, our natural tendency is to release the pressure and then press on the container of anxiety again—an action that's counterproductive, since it looks like nervous fidgeting to an observer.

Observing yourself experiencing anxiety, you will notice that you can identify the presence of anxiety's container only through a feeling of diminishing density in the body tissues surrounding the container. Anxiety feels like an *absence of support*—that your solar plexus is not supporting your upper body as well as it normally does. This really is the essence of anxiety. Because of this, simply pressing on the feeling's container with the weight of your upper body will not work very well. Controlling anxiety therefore requires a somewhat different approach.

**Exercise: Disruption of Anxiety**

Again imagine yourself again at an important job interview or in any other situation in which you feel worried and must suppress your anxiety. Pay particularly close attention to the moment when your anxiety is just getting triggered. It originates from one point, along the solar plexus's midline, deep inside, at the upper wall of the container of anxiety. If you run through the same worry-provoking situation again and again, each time trying to interfere with the container's activation, you'll find that stooping forward only makes your anxiety worse and that keeping your posture straight gives you greater freedom to influence the activation of the container. As you press on the container, keeping your posture upright and slightly arching your upper abdomen forward, you'll be applying pressure with your torso close to the ignition point from behind the container. As a result, the trembling sensation—which your mind interprets as anxiety—will become weaker. When you touch the ignition point itself, your anxiety disappears completely, and this deactivation requires only gentle pressure. When you remember the relief that comes from anxiety's deactivation, this technique will begin to become second nature to you.

It will benefit you to consider another aspect of anxiety—the trembling quality of this emotion—as you attempt to control it. When you straighten your posture in relation to the container of anxiety, you will feel that the trembling is contained within the solar plexus. As you've probably experienced, strong anxiety spreads to other areas of your body—trembling hands, shaking knees, quavering voice. But you can prevent this spread by keeping the area around the container of anxiety as motionless as possible. If you do so, the trembling sensation will become milder because the surrounding tissues are not as susceptible to this vibration, and then turning anxiety off will require even less effort.

**Anger**

Arvin has been working hard at his job for the past four years, but he has never been promoted. He is going to talk to his boss, and he is feeling angry, but he doesn't want his boss to take notice of that, so Arvin carefully suppresses his true feelings.

What is curious about anger in this or a similar situation is that it should never be repressed completely. In Arvin's case, it's his anger that compelled him to talk to his boss in the first place, and if he turns it off completely, he'll lose his motivation to discuss his promotion. What he needs to do is to curb his anger by not letting the feeling fill its container to the point of turning into anger's more intense forms. The sensation of anger needs to stay close to its ignition points. If you observe Arvin, you'll see how he tenses up his ribcage while his posture remains upright or even very slightly arched forward.

**Exercise: Disruption of Anger**

Imagine yourself in Arvin's shoes or in a situation in which you felt angry but had to hide your true feelings, and observe how the container of anger becomes active. Its two ignition points are located near the abdomen's surface, behind your ribcage, one on each side. From these two points, anger spreads deeper into your torso, first directly toward the spine and then encircling the core of your body in layers, until the stimulation fills the two containers all the way to the surface of the front and sides of your abdomen. Because anger's movement has such a strange trajectory, simply pressing its containers with your upper body does not stop its formation; it only redistributes it, a little. The reason why leaning against the containers does not work has to do with the location of the ignition points.

Run the same situation in your mind again, but this time pay attention to the moments before and during the activation of the ignition points. You'll notice that anger's ignition points are activated when you tense up your abdomen and your ribcage around the ignition points. As you can observe yourself, your body weight only barely influences the points' activation. If you flex your abdominal muscles more than you feel the need to during the moment when your anger becomes ignited, then you interrupt the anger's formation. If your effort comes after the feeling's ignition moment, then you simply trap the amount of anger that has already been formed, preventing it from developing any further.

**Fear**

Darrel is strolling in the woods with his friends. There is a wide stream ahead. Darrel's friends jump over it, but Darrel stops. The stream is too wide, and Darrel's previous experience tells him that he might fall into the cold water. While Darrel hesitates, his friends are walking on, leaving him behind. Darrel suppresses his fear and jumps.

In such a situation, Darrel (or anybody else) will probably feel more than just fear. The fear will be accompanied by anxiety and hesitation, but these extraneous feelings appear as a reaction to the fear, and once you deactivate your fear, the anxiety and hesitation will vanish, too. So, for the purpose of this exercise, please disregard any other emotions you may feel, and focus your attention solely on fear.

**Exercise: Disruption of Fear**

Imagine yourself in a situation in which you experienced fear but had to suppress it in order to do something you were afraid of, and observe what happens to the containers of fear. The containers become active and make you straighten your back to the point that it becomes arched backward, mildly paralyzing you and making all the following movements more difficult. The first thing that you instinctively do to release the fear's chilling grip is bend your torso slightly forward. As soon as you feel the constricted containers more pronouncedly, your torso bends forward a couple of degrees more, stretching the back walls of fear's containers.

After you have mentally run through the situation in which you successfully took your fear under control enough times to memorize the movements your mind and body instinctively use to curb its effects and deactivate the feeling, try imagining a situation in which fear took over your consciousness and try applying these same, barely noticeable movements on that situation. If you have practiced enough, you will instinctively prevent your back from straightening to the point of locking the fear in its containers, because the farther this movement goes, the more difficult it becomes to relieve the fear's paralyzing effect. This first movement takes most work. When you get past this first movement, you'll feel compelled to do something in reaction to the fear. Whatever that next movement is, you should feel the backmost boundaries of the fear's containers. Make sure that you keep the back walls of the containers stretched during that next movement. The intensity of the stretch needs to exceed that of impulse to let it constrict, and during the same second movement, the urge to squeeze the containers should subside, turning off your fear.

**Disgust**

Lisa's cat once killed a bird and brought the dead animal to her as a gift, putting it on the floor by Lisa's feet. Lisa felt nausea when she saw the bloody corpse of the little bird, but she couldn't let it lie there, its blood staining the floor, so she took her feelings under control and did some cleaning.

All containers become activated as your mind commands your body to squeeze them. Containers naturally carry on the command, amplifying and holding the constricted state, until a new command orders them to do something else or until the strength of the first constriction wears out. The stronger that first squeeze is, the more powerfully a container will constrict. What is special about the container of disgust is that when it constricts too much, it triggers vomiting. This is why it is particularly important to interfere with disgust's activation during the early stages.

**Exercise: Disruption of Disgust**

Imagine yourself in a situation in which you were able to control your disgust. Observe carefully how your mind and body quarantine the formed disgust. You instinctively straighten your back and push the entire container of disgust forward, thus identifying and slightly stretching its boundaries and interrupting its constriction. Mentally run through several similar situations in which you were naturally able to contain your feeling of disgust, and observe carefully how you did it, until you have identified every stage of this process. When you understand how it works, imagine a situation from your past in which you were so grossed out that you could not control your urge to vomit. Try using the same mechanism that your mind and body employ to contain the feeling of disgust to interrupt this strong repulsion, noting that its disruption requires only a minimal effort during the early stages of the feeling's activation.

On the most general level, you should not let your torso bend forward during the initial stage of disgust's formation, but that is not enough to disrupt an intense disgust. You need to stretch the container of disgust back into the shape it has when dormant; then, your next action will turn off the remainder of your disgust, but the small movements that are essential to carry out this task can only be obtained from your own self-observation.

**Sexual Desire**

John has just started seeing Mary, and thinking about her excites him a great deal, sexually. Now, he is at work, and while John is fantasizing about Mary in arousing situations, he does not notice that his boss is approaching him. His boss's polite question, "How's your project coming along?" explodes in John's distracted mind. "Just fine," he quickly replies as he instinctively leans forward, pressing on his lower abdomen with the entire weight of his upper body. The problem is, this doesn't make his arousal disappear. In fact, his perfectly intuitive action makes the feeling get stuck right where it was.

Remember that the area of sexual desire is not a container. You've got to remember this on an *emotional* level, because your mind and body instinctively treat the area as if it were a container. The difference between an emotion's container and the area of sexual desire is that sexual desire is not *contained* in the area where you feel it; that area merely acts as a switch that turns your entire emotional state to the sexual mode, so leaning against that switch will not help you to turn off your sexual desire.

**Exercise: Disruption of Sexual Desire**

Imagine yourself in a situation in which you got sexually excited and needed to stop your arousal immediately. Your mind and body respond by leaning forward, pressing on the area where you feel your excitement and thus locking it in the state of arousal, making it even more difficult to deactivate.

Even though this movement occurs naturally, it is counterproductive. It simply does not work on sexual desire, which needs to be approached completely differently. The approach you'll use is the opposite of the technique we've been discussing. You'll find it in the section on Technique 3, below.

## Technique 2: Forceful Suppression

Imagine yourself going to the beach on a sunny but windy day. You've brought along a large beach umbrella, which you need to insert in the sand, but you don't want the wind to pull the umbrella out of the sand and send it tumbling across the beach, possibly injuring somebody. As you push the umbrella's metal pole into the sand, you realize that simply pushing the pole into the sand does not produce enough force to secure the umbrella well. The solution that naturally comes to your mind is to twist the umbrella's pole alternately clockwise and then counterclockwise a few times while pushing the pole deeper in the sand. This natural impulse usually produces the desired result: your beach umbrella will be able to withstand a somewhat stronger wind.

The technique of forceful suppression works similarly. Merely by pressing a container with your upper body, you can disrupt emotions that are weak or moderate in strength, but strong emotions require more powerful pressure, which you instinctively produce by twisting the part of your torso located above the active container alternately clockwise and then counterclockwise, usually no more than two times in a row. Due to certain containers' structures or locations, this twisting motion needs to be adjusted—sometimes beyond recognition—just as your movement would if there were a hard object that prevented the umbrella's pole from going any deeper in the sand. You'd have to get creative to set your umbrella securely in the sand, but when it comes to feelings, the creative aspect has already been taken care of, and all you need to do is to identify what your mind and body naturally do to solve the problem for each of the containers. Let us look at this movement in detail, in relation to specific feelings that appear in specific situations.

## Joy

Ray is playing poker, and he gets a great hand. It is unlikely that anyone at the table will be able to beat his hand, which means that the $10,000 at stake will be Ray's. Ray feels that he is about to scream from joy, but he composes himself and without a twitch continues to maintain a sour-puss facial expression until he wins the game.

### Exercise: Disruption of Joy

Picture yourself a situation in which you need to firmly repress an unusually strong emotion of joy. The basic movement is similar to the one that you would use to suppress mild- to moderate-strength joy, but there are three important differences. The first has to do with the tone of the muscles surrounding the container of joy. It becomes much more motionless—like a predator before an attack. This tone allows you to feel the constriction of the container, thus giving you more freedom to act. The second difference is that you bend your upper torso at a sharper angle. Its location depends on the phase at which you decide to stop the emotion from filling its container any further—which needs to be level with the lower part of the container. And the third difference is that the upper torso does not tilt straight forward but twists about one-third of a full turn, clockwise or counterclockwise, while tilting forward and then about one-third of a complete turn in the opposite direction, firmly sealing the forming joy at a whatever phase of development the movement interrupts the emotion.

As with the basic suppression technique, you can apply this pressure closer to joy's ignition point, but if less than one-third of the container has been activated, there is no need for forceful suppression; basic suppression will suffice. Whenever you are pressing directly on the ignition point, a firm touch is all you need to stop the formation of joy.

**Aversion**

Sandy is the owner of an advertising agency. She has not been able to find enough work for all ten of her employees to stay busy, and she knows that she'll have to lay off two of them. She really does not want to do it, but she doesn't have the financial resources to stay in business if she does not downsize her company. She suppresses her aversion, which is her primary reaction to what she is planning to do, and prepares the pink slips.

**Exercise: Disruption of Aversion**

Picture yourself in a situation in which you really did not want to do something, but the circumstances demanded that you had to act contrary to what you felt. If you imagine yourself back in that situation, you will notice that, when forcefully suppressing aversion, your instinct is not to shake your head or twist your chest from side to side but to press sharply and firmly on the part of aversion's container that is located behind the container of joy, so the feeling cannot connect the two compartments of the container. Once the back portion of the container is deactivated, your impulse is to continue pressing on the container against the front wall of your chest, flattening the container as much as possible. When the circumstances call for complete deactivation of aversion, you instinctively lean even more firmly against the container. The tendency in this case is not so much to turn from side to side—as you would with the beach umbrella—but to slide upward across the feeling's ignition points, significantly increasing the pressure on the container in this torso shift. As a result, your shoulders shift forward, wrapping around the container of aversion and managing to touch both of its ignition points, thus turning the emotion off completely.

## Sadness

Amy had been in a relationship with Greg five years. When they broke up, she was angry at him and at herself, but as time passed, the feeling of anger was replaced by grief and loneliness—which has been Amy's emotional state for a few months now. Today, however, Amy needs to make a presentation at a client company, and Amy's boss has asked her to make her presentation cheerful. On the way to the client, she is still sulking, but as she passes through the entrance to client's office building, Amy pulls herself together and squeezes herself into a cheerful mood.

## Exercise: Disruption of Sadness

Imagine yourself in a situation in which it was crucial that you suppress your sadness really well for a certain period, and observe how exactly your mind and body accomplish that.

The inflexible ribcage does not allow you to turn it in relation to the containers of sadness, and as with aversion, you do not twist your chest from side to side but, with a deep sigh, you straighten your back, simultaneously leaning against the feeling's ignition points. Notice how the deep sigh and the straightening of your back push sadness's ignition points forward and upward, making it possible for you to press on them with the front wall of your chest and to hold the pressure with the weight of your head and upper torso. In this posture, the containers of sadness become temporarily isolated and quarantined.

**Anxiety**

Fred is about to be interviewed, and he is fine with that. Well, he *thought* he was fine, until he saw the video camera in the interview room. There is something about being on camera that makes Fred extremely anxious. He starts to sweat, his hands begin to tremble, and he feels he will have difficulty speaking. Fred makes an almost superhuman effort and suppresses his panic attack. His symptoms reluctantly subside.

## Exercise: Disruption of Anxiety

Put yourself in Fred's shoes or imagine yourself in another situation in which it was very important that you suppress your anxiety, and observe how your instincts handle it.

Because there is no ribcage in the middle of your upper abdomen, this area naturally allows a much greater freedom of movement. Observing your innate reaction, you will notice how your upper body—that is, the part of your body that is located above the container of anxiety—sharply shifts forward, leaning against the area of the container in which the emotion has already begun to spread. As soon as the weight of your body blocks the way of the spreading anxiety, you can feel your torso twist once to each side on top of the container, firmly sealing the isolated feeling. Your next instinct will be to keep the area of the seal still throughout the anxiety-provoking situation until the feeling passes.

If you study your instinctive reaction in this sort of situation until you become aware of the many tiny movements that regulate the state of your anxiety, you will be able to simulate identical shifts in your torso to intervene in activation of the feeling. As with all emotions, the earlier you intervene, the less effort it will take to keep your anxiety under control.

**Anger**

Meet Deborah. She is an illustrator by education but now does website design. Her business partner, Alex, has organized a meeting with the executives of a large corporation, and if everything goes well, she will see a significant increase in her income. And everything *had* been going well until she and Alex entered the room in which the meeting was taking place, and Deborah saw her former boyfriend sitting at the conference table. They had gone out for three years, until Deborah discovered that he had cheated on her *and* stolen her money. But what she hated most was that he suddenly disappeared from her life, and she never had a chance to tell the bastard what she really thought of him.

Now, as she enters the room and spies him there, Deborah's rage toward her ex appears and almost immediately consumes her. But given the great importance of this meeting to the future of her and Alex's company, Deborah cannot give her former boyfriend all that he has coming to him! And so Deborah manages to do something that she has never thought she could do: she suppresses her rage and manages to stay calm and professional throughout the entire forty-minute meeting! Later, though, she feels so stressed out that her hands shake and she can hardly speak—but, even so, she did manage to control her anger during that crucial period.

**Exercise: Disruption of Anger**

Now, picture yourself in a similar situation in which you were furious but it was crucial that you did not show even a hint of anger, and watch carefully how your body and mind regulate your emotional state.

Anger's containers' anatomical locations allow you to get a good hold on them by leaning on them with your upper body, thus pressing the containers against the tightened muscles of the upper abdomen. The angrier you are, the clearer you can feel the side-to-side twist that you perform with your upper torso to ensure a leak-proof seal of the containers. Your rage will stop developing at whatever stage you sealed it with this side-to-side torque.

Think of several situations that make you furious, and try applying this innate technique to each of them, but do it during progressively earlier phases of the feeling's formation. Depending on how explosive your temper is, at certain point, you may not need to twist your upper body side to side; a gentle pressure will suffice to stop the anger's development. By experimenting with your anger, you will develop greater skill in controlling the formation of the feeling.

**Fear**

As Angela crosses a road, she is so consumed by her thoughts that she doesn't pay attention to what's going on around her. Suddenly, a car, moving very fast, turns onto the street she is crossing, and it almost strikes her before she realizes what is happening. When she finally becomes aware of the danger of the situation, Angela propels herself out of the car's way.

**Exercise: Disrupting the Formation of Fear**

You've probably been in a situation like the one just described, in which you narrowly missed being hit by a car only because you managed to move out of the way despite your surge of fear. In imagination, place yourself in that situation, and observe how your mind and body allow you to curb your fright and act in spite of it.

Note how the containers of fear fill up instantly, producing a paralysis that stands in the way of the push from your back, making it harder to react. Fright always paralyzes you, and you can experience its immobilizing effect firsthand just by observing your emotional reaction in this imaginary situation. So how do you manage, like Angela, to suppress your fear so quickly?

To have the option of acting quickly, your body needs to squeeze the containers of fear. Your instinct here will be to keep the area of your back in which the containers of fear are located very still. If you were to twist your upper torso—as you do to curb anger, for example—then the containers of fear would widen, further impairing your ability to react. What your body and mind do instead is react to the fright's appearance first and to the approaching car second. As you probably remember from the chapter on the activating breath, you can predict the intensity of the emotion that is about to appear from the intensity of the exhalation that precedes it. In the case of the fright, your body and mind must react to that exhalation—which in itself guarantees that you're about to be frightened—by narrowing the area in your back that fear's containers occupy by pressing on them with your upper torso, which stoops a little forward, and from the sides, by means of your shoulders turning forward and taking the entire flanks with them. The narrowed containers still impair your ability to act but to a significantly lesser degree, and you can jump out of the oncoming car's way.

**Disgust**

Roger had to use a public restroom. Everything was fine, until, while pulling up his pants, Roger accidentally pushed his wallet out of a pocket. As luck would have it, the darned wallet landed not somewhere on the restroom's floor, but right in the middle of the toilet bowl! Roger heard it plunge into the water and then saw it floating there. It took a mere moment for Roger to overcome his disgust. In one swift movement, he reached down into the toilet and pulled out his wallet.

**Exercise: Disruption of Disgust**

Picture yourself in a situation that grosses you out but in which you need to act despite your disgust. You'd better suppress it quickly, or you may throw up! Your instinct is to seal the edges of disgust's container, but you experience no impulse to twist your torso from side to side near the container. This is because the container of disgust is not surrounded by any bones, and if you do twist your body, you will disperse the sensation of disgust, letting it occupy a larger area and thus making it more difficult to contain the emotion. You would also push the back wall of the container a bit forward and tense up the muscles around it, to quarantine the feeling.

**Sexual Desire**

Feel free to experiment with the forceful suppression on your libido, but I can't think of any possible way to make it work. Because of the nature of the area of sexual desire, the forceful suppression technique will only make the sexual arousal worse. In fact, you'll get better results if you don't do anything with it and let the excitement pass on its own.

# Technique 3: Release of Pressure

Imagine children playing in the snow. One boy keeps pushing a snowball across a meadow. The snowball keeps growing as more snow adheres to it, and it takes increasingly more effort for the boy to continue pushing it. Then, his mother's call, "*Danny!*," echoes across the meadow, and the boy turns his head. He suddenly leaves his big snowball where it is and runs off, without even looking back.

You can rarely just abandon something that you do in your life—particularly if that something is important—but you can always take this approach when dealing with feelings. While experiencing emotions is essential to human interaction (people often turn away from you if you're indifferent toward them and their problems or interests), emotions themselves never advance the accomplishment of a goal, and you can always give up a feeling if it begins to get in your way. The approach to controlling feelings that we're going to discuss here is identical to what Danny did with his snowball—you simply abandon the troublesome emotion. The way the technique works in reality is this: You stop squeezing the feeling's container or containers, and that container or containers will go back to the dormant state, thus turning off the emotion.

This technique may seem counterintuitive at first, but it *is* the most effective approach described in this chapter, and your body and mind frequently employ it when situations take an extreme or unwanted emotional turn, because this technique can be used to turn off an emotion of unlimited intensity. So let's look at this technique in relation to each of the containers and areas.

**Joy**

Sam is sitting in his favorite chair at home and watching a movie that he enjoys. Then he suddenly remembers that he's supposed to meet his girlfriend in a few minutes. He's going to be late!

**Naturally Occurring Disruption of Joy**

If you imagine yourself in Sam's situation or a similar one, you can feel how your body and mind deactivate your joy. Notice how Sam suddenly remembers something that requires his full attention, and he has to give up the pleasure that he's experiencing because it occupies too much space in his mind. What I want you to consider here is how, in such a situation, you let go of your joy.

If you think of any situation that triggers joy in you, you'll notice that to experience joy, you must straighten your mid-back. In some instances, you can feel some joy when you're stooped forward a little—but not a full-fledged feeling of joy. If you stoop forward, your joy will be mixed with a little sadness. So why do you need to straighten your back? Observe the very beginning of any situation that makes you giggle or laugh. The ticklish sensation that makes you giggle comes from a delicate but firm pressure—which feels like a tickle—that you apply to the back of the container of joy, which you achieve by straightening your back, thus squeezing the container between the part of your torso that's located behind the container and the chest wall in front of the container. The degree of this pressure is amazingly precise, because it determines how strong your joy will be, and it stays stable throughout a given joyous phase. When Sam instinctively turns off his joy, he merely releases that pressure on the container.

**Exercise: Disruption of Joy**

Jane smokes about half a pack of cigarettes a day, and she has been trying to quit for a few years. She's had no success, so far. Every time she decides to stop smoking, she takes her decision seriously and doesn't even touch cigarettes for a while, but then something always happens that shakes her up emotionally, and she finds herself smoking, again.

All bad habits—not just smoking—produce joy (or, rather, comfort, which is a form of joy), making the ability to manipulate the container of joy an important skill to have. For this exercise, choose any bad or useless habit you may have, and observe your emotions while you are indulging in the habit. Do you feel the container of joy being slightly activated? To produce the feeling of comfort, the pressure on the container of joy is mild, and you need to identify it clearly. Pay particularly close attention to the very beginning of the feeling activation, when you're just touching the back wall of the container. For this exercise, you're going to need a real habit—it won't work with an imaginary one. Remember a time when you wanted to indulge your habit, but *don't* let yourself press on the container. Stay absolutely still during this instant when you feel compelled to touch the container. If you still feel even the slightest impulse to follow your habit, it means that you need to stay still during an earlier moment, because if you don't make any attempt to press on the container at all, your desire to indulge your habit will remain dormant. Run through several situations from your memory in which your habit controlled your actions, but stay still during the moment when the feeling of comfort generated by the habit is about to start—don't even twitch. After several days of such practice, you'll develop a final say over whether you want the comfort associated with your habit turned on or not. If your response is be a definite *no*, which manifests itself in stillness when the possibility comes up, then the feeling of comfort associated with the habit will gradually subside. Oftentimes, when comfort disappears, the feeling of aversion fills in the empty spot in the emotional state.

**Aversion**

Once, I stopped by the house of some friends—a young couple with a baby girl—and witnessed the following scene: The girl's mother was trying to feed her baby, but the girl kept whining and turning away from the spoon. Then the mother found a brilliant solution to the problem: She placed one green pea on the top of a spoonful of baby food that she was giving to the girl, and the baby stared at the pea with her mouth open.

The feeling of aversion made the little girl twist her torso to turn away from the spoon, but the green pea attracted her interest, and the girl's mind turned off her feeling of aversion.

**Naturally Occurring Disruption of Aversion**

Ben needs to take a business trip to a small town he's never heard of, and he really doesn't want to go. Ben complains about the trip to his best friend, and his friend decides to join him. A few hours later, two more friends have said they'll go along, too. The dreaded business trip has now become a pleasure trip, as well, and when Ben thinks about it, he no longer feels aversion; he feels excitement.

In this example, the chief feeling in Ben's emotional state shifts from aversion to joy (excitement being a form of joy). Ben's mind turns off his aversion to the trip by making his body release the pressure on the container of aversion and apply it to the container of joy. We already know how to squeeze the container of joy, but let's analyze how the pressure is applied to the container of aversion and how it can be controlled.

## Exercise: Disruption of Aversion

Imagine yourself in a situation in which your mind turned off your reluctance to do something, and observe how your mind and body accomplished that.

Whenever you experience the feeling of aversion, your body applies pressure to the sides of the container of aversion by turning your shoulders slightly forward and down. This is why babies that don't want to do something often twist their torsos from side to side: they feel squeezed from the sides, and they're trying to get out from that—quite physical—pressure. Twisting, however, is not an effective way to get rid of that uncomfortable feeling. One of the best ways to deactivate your aversion completely is not to let it appear at all. As when you wanted to prevent joy from appearing, you shouldn't let your body even begin pressing on the container. So while running some situations that trigger your aversion through your mind, you need to observe the very beginning of the feeling's appearance and also the moments just before the aversion's activation. Don't even twitch during those initial moments. After a few days of practicing this, you'll develop a final say over whether or not you want your aversion to be turned on. If you do this exercise perfectly, then instead of aversion, your joy should step in, because aversion and joy always function in tandem with each other.

## Sadness

A neighbor with whom Lily was friendly called Lily one day and told her that her dog had just been run over by a car. Lily felt sorrow explode and fill the sides of her chest as he described the details of the accident, the gruesome extent of the dog's injuries, and the agony of its death. Then, to Lily's shock, he admitted that he was playing a prank on her. Lily glanced at the calendar and saw that it was April Fools' Day. Her rage appeared just as quickly as her sadness vanished, and she proceeded to tell her neighbor just what she thought of his cruel joke, using language that we're not going to repeat here.

Lily released the pressure on the containers of sadness because she needed all her strength to give her so-called friend all that he deserved, but for our purposes here, let's focus on how she released the pressure on the containers of sadness.

## Naturally Occurring Disruption of Sadness

You experience various forms of the same emotion when you apply pressure to different areas of that emotion's container's outer surfaces. This is particularly true with the containers of sadness. Among all the containers of emotions, sadness's two containers have the largest surface area, and so they allow many shades of sorrow: disappointment, nostalgia, the feeling of loss, and so on. Usually, however, activation of the containers of sadness requires comparatively more pressure applied to a larger area than does the activation of other feelings. The pressure comes from slouching the back and turning the shoulders forward and down. When the pressure is released, the back straightens and the shoulders turn outward and backward. Very subtle movements, however, can play a crucial role, because the body language associated with sadness is not always clearly visible, even when sadness is present.

## Exercise: Disruption of Sadness

Picture yourself being cruelly tricked on April Fools' Day or in any other situation in which your mind abruptly turns off your sadness, and observe how this process occurs.

A sudden onset of sadness usually involves a slight forward tilt of the head and a tightening of muscles in the shoulders and upper back. Then, later, if the emotion isn't deactivated, many of the involved muscled begin to tire. Your body and mind then begin to substitute the squeezing effect of the muscles surrounding the containers with the weight of the head and arms—this switch occurs naturally when you slouch—thus applying the identical degree of pressure that earlier came from the constricted muscles. As you did in the disruption of joy and aversion, put your observational efforts into analyzing what is going on immediately before your sadness appears. When you've identified the torso movements that trigger your sadness, run through the same situation in your mind again, but this time exclude these movements from your reaction. Don't allow the involved areas to quiver even slightly. If you do this well, you should feel no sadness in this imaginary situation. Try identifying and then excluding the torso movements that press on the containers of sadness in several more imagined situations or in situations drawn from your past, and see if the sad component can be completely removed from your emotional reaction. If you repeat this exercise enough times, you'll have a choice whether to experience sadness in a given situation or leave it in its dormant state.

## Anxiety

Ann is scheduled to give a speech in fifteen minutes, and she is anxiously reviewing her notes. Then, ten minutes before she's to go on stage, she's suddenly informed that due to some technical problems, her speech is being cancelled. Ann did not know that she was worried until she heard the news and felt her anxiety subside.

## Naturally Occurring Disruption of Anxiety

The container of anxiety seems to collapse under pressure. All other containers produce an almost dense quality, a sensation of firmness that's a reaction to being squeezed by the surrounding muscles, and this firm quality of the sensation in the containers brings to life the emotion you're experiencing. The container of anxiety, however, behaves differently. It swallows the pressure that's being applied to it. The more you squeeze it, the more you'll feel the sensation of a hole within yourself. On the one hand, your mind makes your body react this way in situations where you're responsible for the outcome, but on the other, your mind interprets the sensation of a hole in your solar plexus as a reason for panic. For this reason, it's particularly important to apply your efforts to observing the very instant when anxiety is triggered. If you don't intervene at the initial stages of the feeling's activation, controlling it becomes increasingly difficult.

**Exercise: Disruption of Anxiety**

Imagine yourself in Ann's place or in a similar situation in which a turn of events shut down your anxiety, and observe the movement that occurs around your solar plexus.

Two things are going on that affect your anxiety. The first is the muscle tension that pushes the front wall of your upper abdomen inward, toward your back. The second is the tilt of your body that's located above your solar plexus forward. These two movements squeeze the container of anxiety from front and back, and each of these movements requires separate attention.

As you think of a situation that made you worry, carefully observe the increase in muscle tension in your upper abdomen at the very beginning of your anxiety's onset. Your goal is to identify the relationship between this tension and the emotional shift from the comfort you feel during the moment before the feeling appears and the state of anxiety that follows it. What's unusual about this muscle tension is that it's directed at the small area in the center of your solar plexus. Don't fight that movement; just don't permit it to start at all. To do so, you need to stay absolutely still during the moments before the situation triggers your anxiety and to keep your abdominal muscles in the state that they are in before the anxiety appears. Once you've managed not to let the muscle tension enter the picture, move on, in your imagination, to other situations in which you felt worried, and exclude that muscle tension from the feeling formation. When you begin to feel comfortable in separating this muscle tension from the rest of the movements, then you can start working on the upper body's tilt forward.

Imagine yourself in Ann's situation again—at the moment when she learns her speech has been cancelled—but this time, observe what's going on with your posture. Your upper body moves slightly backward, yes? When you've identified this movement clearly, cross-check it against other worrisome situations from your memory. As you observe your torso's movements in relation to each of these situations, you'll see that your torso leans forward every time—but to different degrees. Once you've clearly identified this forward tilt's role in the appearance of your anxiety, run through the same situations again, but this time don't allow your body to lean forward. Again, don't fight the movement; just don't let it start. When you become comfortable excluding this tilt from the formation of anxiety, run through the same series of situations yet again, but this time around exclude the muscle tension *together* with the tilt forward. Once you have extracted these two movements from a number of worry-inducing situations from your memory and imagination, you'll learn how to turn off your anxiety in many anxiety-producing situations. And as you repeatedly use this technique in real-life situations, your skill in using it will become greater and greater.

**Fear**

Bob cannot understand how his friends managed to persuade him to go sky diving. It had seemed like a joke to him until his friends started jumping out of the airplane's open door, disappearing into the air. As he watches them—and his own turn approaches—Bob feels a jolt of fear paralyzing his legs and making his breathing difficult and shallow. But Bob knows it's too late for him to back down now. He waddles a few steps forward and the cold, powerful wind scoops him away into the blue sky.

When your fear becomes excessive but you really want to do something in spite of it, your mind and body release their grip on the container and allow you to act as you will.

**Naturally Occurring Disruption of Fear**

Because of fear's containers' location, movements of the torso do not have much effect on fear's activation. Fear's activation does make you straighten your back, but this movement is actually secondary to the feeling's activation process, because the movement is limited by the ribcage in the back of your torso. The main and essential component of fear's appearance is a cramp-like tightening of muscles in your back, around the containers. Controlling this muscle constriction is very similar to controlling your bowels and can be learned only via repeated attempts.

**Exercise: Disruption of Fear**

Imagine that you're at home going through your bills and preparing to pay them, when you suddenly hear a loud thump right behind you. You quickly turn around and see that a thick book has fallen to the floor.

Carefully observe the sensations that you instinctively interpret as being startled. You most likely straightened your back, but focus your attention on what made you straighten your back. If you miss it, don't worry. In this imaginary situation, when you look around and see that the noise was caused by a book falling to the floor, your realization somehow signals your mind to release fear's grip, and you can feel the feeling subside. Notice the relaxation of the muscles that produced your feeling of being startled. When these muscles cramp up, they compel you to straighten your torso. Once you've clearly identified the involved muscles, run through the same situation in your mind again, but this time don't allow these muscles to contract—it takes some mental effort, but it's not all that difficult. You need to keep the area around the containers still only for a brief moment when a specific impulse urges them to contract. When you manage to isolate that impulse via staying still, you'll have the final decision over whether or not to be startled. After you've accomplished this, you should be able to control your fear, as long as it doesn't get much stronger.

To control a stronger fear, think back to the example of Bob's skydiving. Imagine yourself in this situation or one in which you experienced a similarly intense fear, and observe carefully how the fright's activation takes place. Stronger fears involve the same muscles, but they contract more powerfully and include wider areas around the containers. The exercise remains the same: first, identify these muscles via observation; second, run through the situation again, but force the muscles to stay motionless, not allowing the impulse that initializes your fright to make them contract. Try this exercise on many situations from your memory and imagination, trying to eliminate every little twitch related to the fear's appearance. Gradually, controlling your fear will become second nature to you, just as controlling your bowels has become.

**Disgust**

Marcy has been given a funny-looking fruit. She had smelled its gut-wrenching odor from a distance, but now, as she takes it in her hands, the stench becomes almost unbearable. But she makes a superhuman effort not to vomit, and she tastes the fruit. To her amazement, it's delicious. For a moment, Marcy forgets about the nauseating aroma and savors the flavor.

**Naturally Occurring Disruption of Disgust**

Whenever you encounter something disgusting, your body stoops forward, but just as when you straighten your back when fear is being turned on, this is just a secondary effect. The abdominal muscles contract toward the container, locking it like a clenching hand. If you don't stop its activation at the very beginning, disruption of disgust at a later stage becomes exponentially more difficult—like stopping a muscle cramp.

**Exercise: Disruption of Disgust**

This is one of a few instances where imagination doesn't do a good job recreating a feeling. It's very difficult to imagine a situation in such a lifelike way that can actually gross you out. It's therefore much easier to recreate the feeling of disgust if you turn to visual or olfactory "props" for reinforcement. Do you find spiders, worms, or centipedes disgusting? If so, try to summon your disgust by looking at some images or video footage of the repulsive creatures, observing the sensations you feel. You'll most likely feel only small muscle contractions, like "butterflies" below your stomach, and you may feel your abdomen rumble. Now, distract yourself with something else until the feeling fades away, then look at the gross picture again, but this time try to keep your whole abdomen as still as you can. This part of the exercise will help you to isolate the impulse that triggers your reaction and thus allow you to decide whether or not to allow this reaction of repulsion to occur. When you become comfortable with shutting down a mild feeling of disgust, begin working on more powerful nausea-provoking images or smells.

**Sexual Desire**

Phil was staying with his parents, but they were going to be out for the evening, so when his girlfriend Kate came over to see him, he and she felt safe having sex on the living room sofa. They'd just begun, however, when Phil's mother and father came home unexpectedly, catching Phil and Kate with their pants down, literally. After that embarrassing incident, Phil did not want to have sex for a while.

Notice that there are two parts to the emotional shift that Phil lived through. The first is the embarrassment he felt; the second one is the deactivation of his sexual desire.

## Naturally Occurring Disruption of the Sexual Desire

Activation of sexual desire involves a slight tilt of the pelvis forward. This movement is like that of a pendulum—forward and up. The increase in muscle tension in the lower abdomen, however, plays a more important role in sexual desire's activation. It starts from two points located about two finger-breadths below the navel and a hand-width to each side of the abdominal midline, but, as sexual desire strengthens, it involves nearly the entire lower abdomen.

Imagine yourself in Phil's place or any other situation in which a sudden shock made you lose your sexual desire, and observe how your mind turns it off. The pendulum-like swing forward allows your abdominal muscles to contract so they press on two points, one on each side of your lower abdomen, about three fingers below and a hand's-width to each side of your navel, thus activating the sexual area. Then, when you experience a shock, your mind releases the muscle tension and lets go of the pelvic tilt. Imagine yourself in several such situations with various degree of sexual arousal, and try to disrupt it at various stages. The technique is the same for any degree of arousal, and but it dissolves faster if you switch to a different emotion, particularly anxiety. You may find it helpful to study this process for either disruption or regulation of sexual arousal; the technique remains the same, but it becomes more fine-tuned.

## Summary

The most natural and intuitive approach to emotional control is to suppress emotions. It's also the worst way to regulate one's feelings, because repression of emotion requires a significant amount of energy, and when you suppress an emotion for a while and spend a lot of energy doing so, the emotion tends to return at even greater strength. If modified, however, this approach can be used to turn off emotions as well as repress them. For our discussion, we extracted three techniques from this natural approach: (1) basic suppression, (2) forceful suppression, and (3) release of pressure.

In most cases, the basic suppression of feelings involves leaning against the emotion's container with your upper body and pressing it with the surrounding muscles. The general rule is that it takes less effort to repress a feeling if you press on the container at a place closer to emotion's ignition point(s). Every feeling has either one or two ignition points (one if the emotion has only one container; two if the feeling has two symmetrical containers on the right and left sides of the torso). These are the points from which emotions originate and begin to fill their containers. Joy's ignition point is located near the bottom of its single container, and suppression of this feeling is achieved by a tilt of the upper torso and head forward. Aversion's ignition points are located in the lower third of the container, one on each side of the container of joy, and aversion's suppression is accomplished by turning the shoulders forward and down. Sadness's ignition points are found in the upper third of each of its containers, and the body and mind suppress this feeling by straightening the posture and turning the shoulders up and backward. Anxiety's single ignition point is located deep in the solar plexus, and its repression consists of leaning forward as well squeezing the container by contracting the muscles that surround it. Leaning forward has very little effect on anger's two ignition points, which are located closer to the front surface of the ribcage, and its repression relies mostly on abdominal muscle contraction. Fear's two ignition points are in a similar situation: the ribcage allows only limited movement, and most of the feeling's suppression comes from muscular contraction. The single ignition point of disgust is located deep in the abdomen, and leaning forward doesn't control its activation at all if there's no well-coordinated muscle contraction around the container. Despite being instinctual, suppressing feeling works counterproductively when it comes to sexual desire; if you press on the area of sexual desire with your upper body, you'll actually diminish your body's ability to regulate its state.

The forceful suppression technique works nearly identically to the basic suppression. The only difference is the effort to suppress a feeling is applied more abruptly, forcefully, and to a more specific place in a container or an area. This technique is often marked by a twisting movement from side to side, which helps your body seal a feeling like a cork in a bottle.

In both basic and forceful suppression, the techniques are derived from observation of remembered or imagined situations in which feelings were suppressed, paying particular attention to the very beginning of the reaction to repress a feeling.

The technique of pressure release is the most valuable and effective of the three approaches. Essentially, this technique involves a release of pressure on the container of an emotion, thus allowing you to turn off even an exceptionally powerful and gripping emotion. To learn this technique, you need to observe the movements of your torso that occur moments before an emotion appears. The key to learning this technique is to mentally run through a great many situations that trigger an unwanted emotional response and to stay perfectly still during the initial stage of each feeling's activation. The result will be a disassociation between the mind's emotional reaction and the torso movements that ordinarily accompany it.

# CHAPTER 4: EMOTIONS AND GOAL SETTING

Ever since high school, Dave, a friend of mine, had wanted to become a physician. After graduating from college, Dave spent four years at medical school. It was very hard work, but he passed all his classes and exams, and then, as he was getting close to graduation, Dave realized that his choice of profession was a mistake. When he got his diploma, he did not apply for any residencies (residency is an absolute requirement if you want to become a physician). Instead, he started his own business. About a decade has passed, but there has been nothing in Dave's behavior to indicate any regret about his giving up on his former dream.

Another friend of mine, Josh, also wanted to become a medical doctor. He finished a four-year college and entered medical school. Unfortunately, Josh failed Step 2 of the national board exam several times in a row and, consequently, was not accepted to any residency. Seven years have passed, but Josh's emotional wound still remains fresh.

Somehow Dave's mind managed to turn off the feelings that connected to his dream of becoming a doctor, while Josh's mind failed to do so. Why the difference? To find out, let us look into the phenomenon of "having a dream"—which in this book we are going to call *goal setting*—and see whether you can control this mechanism intentionally.

## What Keeps the Dream Alive?

Have you ever noticed that some of your wishes and desires dissipate over time? You still remember that you had them—and that they were intense at some point in the past—but these memories no longer trigger any emotions in you. By the same token, you've probably also had unfulfilled wishes and desires that, when you think of them now, still cause you strong feelings of sadness, anger, or anxiety. Despite the length of time that has passed, your feelings do not seem to become any weaker. Why? What makes some wishes and desires become mere memories to which no feelings are attached while others retain the power to affect you emotionally?

The force that stands behind persistent emotions is generated by *goals*. As long as you have a set goal for yourself and that goal remains alive—no matter whether you've achieved it or not—there will always be feelings attached to it. On the other hand, if you've changed your mind about certain goals that you had once been passionate about, those *former* goals no longer excite an emotional response in you. Let's look at the goal-setting process in more detail:

Picture yourself waiting for a bus. According to the timetable, the bus should have been here twenty-four minutes ago! If you're like many people, you're probably feeling restless. But why are you so agitated? Your restlessness surely will not make the bus arrive any sooner. In fact, your feelings—no matter what they are—will have no effect on the bus's arrival. So why are you working yourself up into such a state? The reason has to do with the goal or goals you have already set for yourself—the things you intend to accomplish when the bus takes you where you're going. When you have a goal, your body pushes you toward accomplishing it. But when you're just sitting at a bus stop waiting for the bus to arrive, you can't do anything to move closer to accomplishing the goals you've set. Even so, your body keeps pushing you. You grow restless. It's your body's and mind's instinct to make you *do* something—and it literally shakes you up.

By nature, your mind sets numerous goals even without your knowing. You can clearly see this process at work in children and teenagers. Imagine your little boy is playing with other kids at a playground, and then it's time to go home—but your son does not want to go. When you make him leave the playground, he resists you and starts crying. As children grow older, they don't cry as often; they begin to argue instead. Imagine that you tell your teenage son to do his math homework, but he does not feel like doing it. He has a different goal—texting his friends, playing a video game, or whatever. So in response to your telling him to do his homework, he'll say, "Why do I have to do it?" or "What do I need this stupid math for, anyway?" or something of that sort.

Well, as you grow older, your mind still works the same way. The only difference is that you do not cry (well, maybe quietly, when nobody is looking) and only rarely argue; you skillfully suppress your true desires with a sigh, and then you do whatever it is that you are expected to do with a greater or lesser degree of disappointment or irritation.

Ever since childhood, you—like everybody else—have routinely set goals for yourself and tried to accomplish them. And whenever somebody expects you to do something that you yourself haven't planned, your first response is one of reluctance because this is not *your* goal but somebody else's. As you live your life, you learn to take other people's interests into consideration, but you do so only because it might advance fulfillment of your own goals.

Understanding the goal-setting process is an important aspect of learning to control your emotions. Think of your relation to your job. Every day you have to wake up at certain time, which is usually much earlier than you would prefer, so that you can be at your workplace on time—so that you can do things that *somebody else* wants you to do. If you generally enjoy what you do, then using the simple technique of identifying the activating breath and inhaling more than you need to may be enough to allow you to alter any bothersome feelings about work and keep you relatively happy. But if you really despise your work, so much so that doing your job feels like an agonizing, everlasting torture to you, then you are going to need to learn more about the goal-setting process. By applying this knowledge, you'll be able to eliminate or, at least, significantly diminish the annoyance, boredom, or disappointment that arises from your unfulfilled dreams. To control these feelings you may have to intervene not only into the emotions' formation processes but, more important, into the goal-setting process itself, which keeps your feelings alive. And to do that, you'll need to observe the goal-setting process within yourself.

## The Goal-Setting Process

Remember how, at the beginning of this book, I told you that when people daydream, they tend to look up and lean back? Daydreamers behave this way for two reasons: they need to "stay out of the way" of the push that originates right above their lower back—the place where all our dreams and desires start out—and they need to "see" their dream, which causes them to look up, toward the location of the mind's eye.

Daydreaming, however, is always accompanied by the feeling of comfort, which hardly needs an alteration, emotion-wise. What often do need alteration are the emotions accompanying small, everyday goals. Because ordinary chores—cooking, eating, drinking, cleaning, shopping, and many others—involve goal setting, and because of their great number, they form a dense network of goals, the one that we call *routine*. The routine occupies a huge portion of your mind, oftentimes leaving no mental space for the big goals that are much dearer to you. The formation of these mundane goals is nearly identical to how you set your big goals, the ones that you daydream about. What is so special about these small goals is that you fulfill them on regular basis, which, unfortunately, does not happen nearly as often with your big goals. The fact that these small goals are realized many times a day makes them perfect subjects for our exercises in this chapter. So let us look deeper into their mechanisms, using an example:

Meet Paul. Paul is a graduate student working on his dissertation in computer science. Being a scientist, he spends a lot of his time thinking. And when he thinks, he often forgets about other, more mundane things. Now, Paul is in his dormitory room, bending over a notebook, in which he has, for the past four hours, been trying to solve a math problem related to his dissertation. All of a sudden, he looks up, jumps from the stool he's been sitting on, and rushes from the room. What's happened? Well, if we could peer into Paul's mind, we'd see that he has suddenly remembered that he's doing his laundry—and that it's been four hours since he loaded his dirty clothes into a washing machine. He'd completely forgotten about it!

While he rushes to the laundry room to take care of his forgotten laundry, let us review what he has just lived through:

Several hours ago, when Paul decided to do the wash, he had already done it *in his mind.* He saw the real-life image of his dirty clothes, which impressed itself in his mind, and then turned it mentally into the image of clean clothes. Paul accomplished this metamorphosis by activating the emotional response that he would have if his clothes were already clean, which, in turn, triggers the push from the back. This push is what makes the mental image stable, thus setting a goal. When he actually started washing his clothes, he was already behind schedule *mentally*. This holds true with everything that people do. Throughout your life, your body always drags behind your mind. As soon as you make any decision, that goal is instantly accomplished in your thoughts. And your mind does not just accomplish goals immediately; it also accomplishes them *impeccably*, which is nearly *never* the case with a real-life situation.

The lock clicks, and the door opens. Here is Paul coming back into his dorm room, carrying his laundry. Someone had taken it out of the washing machine and put it on the laundry-folding table. Paul had to dry and fold the whole load, which took another hour. Now

Paul looks tired but satisfied. It is the same satisfaction that he experienced when he thought about doing his laundry several hours ago. His actions have caught up with his mind, for now.

Whenever you set a goal, you immediately develop an emotional reaction to that goal. While you can separately deactivate each feeling that you do not want to experience using the techniques that we have already discussed, you can also turn off the entire emotional response by deactivating the goal that triggered that particular emotional reaction. In order to deactivate any emotional response, however, you will first need to know how to intervene in the goal-setting process.

While you can intervene in the goal-setting process at different stages using various approaches, I am going to describe four of the most effective techniques I know: (1) halting the push from the back, (2) giving the push from the back a boost, (3) redirecting the push along an alternate route, and (4) controlling the push via facial expressions.

## Technique 1: Halting the Push

The natural manifestation of this technique is in ignorance. Yes, ignorance usually is not a desirable quality, but if you can use it deliberately to tune out unwanted feelings, then ignorance may become bliss. But before you try to control your ignorance, let's observe how ignorance acts naturally and identify its mechanism.

I remember once seeing Eric, the son of my coworker, playing a computer game while his mom, who hates seeing her son wasting his time, kept asking Eric questions that were meant to distract him and push him toward a productive endeavor. "Did you do your homework?" she asked him. "Yes, mom," Eric replied. "Did you clean your room?" she asked him after a couple of minutes. "Yes, I did," Eric instantly answered. During the hour that Eric spent playing the computer game, his mother asked him several more questions and heard immediate positive responses, many of which were lies. What was curious about this verbal interaction between the mother and her son was that her monotonous questions did not bother Eric; he simply did not care. But how did Eric manage to ignore his mother's slow and irritating assault on his playing the computer game? Well, let's see.

The images that Eric saw on the computer screen excited positive feelings in his mind and body; otherwise he would have stopped playing the game. This means that his feelings were strong enough to trigger the push from his back, which kept Eric's attention glued to the computer screen. A small part of Eric's consciousness was set to "answering-machine mode"—that is, to reply positively to any question that his mother would ask him. Apparently, his mother had been using this strategy for a while, because her son had obviously developed immunity to her approach and remained calm. If you do not have such immunity but want to intentionally ignore somebody's attempts to distract you, then there are a couple of things to consider.

Suppose you are at home working on an important report that you need to finish today, so you can present it to your boss tomorrow, but you have two small children who are bored and want to play with you. You don't particularly enjoy what you are doing, which means that you're already mildly irritated, but when the kids keep distracting you, you don't feel the strength to continue working on your report, and you begin playing with the children, so they'll be quiet—at least for a while! Let's see what can be done to take these emotions under control.

What keeps you working on your report is your sense of responsibility. In other words, it is not your positive feelings that make you work on it but your intention, or, more exactly, a collective intention of yours, your boss's, and that of the organization you work for—because this report needs to be done right and on time! If you observe the sensations in your torso carefully while you're working on your report, you will notice that the container of anger is active. (For comparison, when you do something that you enjoy, the container of anger stays dormant.) This means that whenever something distracts you from your work, you will feel irritated. Your irritation is a mixture of anger and anxiety. Anxiety appears because something interferes with your attempts to achieve your goal, which, as we've already discussed, was achieved mentally within the instant during which you agreed to do the project.

For the technique of halting the push (or selectively ignoring) to be successful—which in this case involves halting the push that makes you put aside your work in order to play with the kids—the first phase of your exercise is to turn off your irritation. But remember that irritation is a combination of anger and anxiety. It's important that you do not try to deactivate your anger, or you will lose the feeling that motivates you to go on working on the report. Instead, focus your efforts solely on the anxiety. When you turn your anxiety off, you will be able to continue working on your report (or whatever you need to do in a given situation).

## Exercise: Turning Off Feelings Using a Dummy Goal

In this exercise you'll use a "dummy goal." That dummy goal needs to be something that you enjoy: it can be your upcoming vacation, working on a hobby you enjoy, or something else that you like. But do not forget that this goal will just be a dummy: Even though you'll hold it in your mind's eye, you'll actually be *thinking* about something else—namely, a task that you must do but don't want to. This is how it works:

Decide to do something that you must do but that you do not like doing—for example, ironing. (Definitely choose something else if, for some reason, you enjoy this tedious and boring task.) As you perform this task, make the goal that you enjoy occupy your entire mind's eye, while letting your *thinking* concentrate on the task at hand. (Otherwise you might injure yourself!) Try this technique on progressively more unpleasant tasks—that is, the ones that you really hate doing—for example, washing dishes (if you, indeed, hate it). If you hold the image of your favorite goal firmly enough, your mind and body will be under the impression that you are actually working on the goal that you see in the middle of your lower forehead.

The purpose of this exercise is to teach yourself to hold the dummy goal—the goal you like—in your mind's eye for increasingly longer periods of time. You can even train yourself to keep such a dummy goal before you, in your mind's eye, for your entire workday, although, if your work requires much thinking, then you will have to train yourself to keep only the *feeling* that the dummy goal produces—that of enjoyment, Remember, it is the sensations that keep you happy, not the mental image, so you can clear your mind's eye whenever you need to. When you become accustomed to this technique, then having the mental image of your goal will not even be necessary. The comfort that the dummy goal produces is the key this technique, and not the goal itself.

If you've never done anything similar to turning off a feeling using a dummy goal, it may remind you the phenomenon of self-delusion. If it does, then you're right. It hardly should be a surprise, though, considering that what we're doing in this book is tracking down the ways your mind and body manipulate your emotional states. Self-delusion is one of many such manipulations. Before you go on, however, there is something that you need to be aware of: Whenever delusions appear on their own, their appearances are not triggered by your intentional effort, and thus they can lead to undesirable effects or even physical or psychological injuries. When you take over the process of delusions' appearances, you do so to achieve a certain goal, and that goal is what keeps you in sound mind.

## Alternative Approach to Technique 1: Turning off Feelings without a Goal

The technique that we're about to look at is also based on something that happens naturally. Picture the following scenario: Timmy, a seven-year-old boy, was running around the apartment's living room with a toy airplane until he knocked over a vase. His mother heard the sound of something breaking, and she rushed into the living room and saw the shattered vase.

"How many times have I told you not to run in the apartment?" was the sentence with which she opened her lecture. Timmy listened to his mom's entire monologue without ever raising his eyes. Periodically, he shook his head. The reason why he did not raise his eyes had in part to do with the fact that he was ashamed to look at his mother. He also instinctively avoided looking at the mental image of himself breaking the vase, because he did not like it; it made him feel uncomfortable. And he shook his head because that is an effective method of temporarily distracting your mind from an unwanted mental image. The meaning of *mind sight*, which basically is your ability to perceive mental images, becomes clearer if you imagine yourself in a similar situation.

**Getting to Know Your Mind Sight**

I am sure you remember yourself breaking something when you were a child, and then getting caught. Do you remember the feeling of discomfort you felt when your parents gave you the kind of lecture that Timmy had to listen to? That discomfort comes as a reaction to the mental picture that already exists in your mind, and your mind is compelling you to look up. And your parents knew about it (from their own experiences, no doubt), because when they asked you, "Did you do that?" and they looked into your eyes, some feeling forced you to respond. (Whether or not you told the truth does not matter, in this case.) But how, exactly, does your mind create this discomfort?

When you or the situation that you are in summons a particular mental image—no matter what that image is—you feel vibration in your solar plexus (a kind of anxiety), which attracts your attention, and you look up to see what is in your mind's eye, thus switching your emotional state. This vibration in your solar plexus serves as a signal every time something in the surrounding environment attracts your attention . The goal, however, will be set only when you look up—that is, when you shift your inner sight away from observing what is in front of you and upward in the direction of your lower forehead. This happens because the push from your lower back always aims at the middle of your lower forehead, and if you don't look up, the push never reaches its destination, thus never stabilizing the emotional state that comes with a given goal.

For example, suppose you are strolling down a street, and you are trying to come up with an idea for a paper that you need to write for a class that you are taking. You are considering a couple of possible ideas, and you are looking downward, a few steps ahead of your feet. Then suddenly, you have a really great idea for your paper—something you have not thought of until this moment—and you look up. Besides enabling you to watch where you are going, keeping your eyes down really helps you think. That is because, when you look down, your thoughts can spin in your mind really fast. When you come across an idea that strikes you as the one that you have been looking for, you look up, and that movement of your eyes stops the rotation of your mind, using the push from your back to pin your idea to the mind's eye, so you will not lose that idea. But let us see how you can use this phenomenon to interfere with an emotion's formation.

**Exercise: Letting Your Mind Spin**

Imagine that you are about to have a meeting with someone whom, for whatever reason, you dislike. Notice that your aversion to that person becomes stronger and more stable immediately after you feel a push from your back, which takes place instantly after you look at your mind's eye—in other words, after you look up *mentally*—and see an image of that person there. Now distract yourself with other thoughts, so the image of that person disappears from your mind. Then think about that person again, but this time, do not raise your inner eyes, do not shift your mind sight. You will feel a vibration in your solar plexus, indicating that the mental image that you requested has appeared—disregard it, or turn the feeling off using any of the techniques that you have learned in the previous chapters. Your aversion to that person should remain just as fleeting as many other thoughts and feelings and should likewise quickly disappear.

You can stop any feeling if you simply do not look at the mind's eye whenever a mental image that triggers unwanted emotions appears there, but the irritation in your solar plexus will be stronger whenever the situation that you are involved in is real instead of imaginary. Once you develop a conscious final say whether or not you want to look up in any imaginary situation, this ability will automatically pass over to real-life situations, too.

## Technique 2: Giving the Push from the Back a Boost

This is how the push from the back occurs naturally: Imagine yourself sitting in a café, sipping coffee, and thinking about something. A woman of about your age comes up to you and insists that you have met before. You are sure that the woman has mistaken you for someone else, but then she tells you your correct name and the name of the school you went to. You look at her carefully. Of course! How could you have forgotten her—you went to school together!

Observe your feelings. An unknown woman is approaching and talking to you. On the emotional level, your mind interprets the sound of her voice and her physical movement toward you similarly to how it interprets an appearance of a mental image, compelling you to look up. The push from your back stabilizes your emotional reaction to the situation that you are in. And this reaction of yours remains stable, until you recognize the woman. When your memory finds the right mental picture to corroborate what the woman is saying, a new push from your back alters your emotional response, while the situation itself remains absolutely the same. This kind of modifying boost to an already formed pattern of feelings can be artificially recreated. And while the naturally occurring boost can activate either positive or negative emotions, it is much easier to intentionally reproduce an additional push that makes you experience comfortable feelings—those akin to satisfaction—than unpleasant ones.

**Getting to Know the Boost**

Take a simple crossword puzzle and try to solve one of the clues. As you read the clue and examine the corresponding line of empty boxes in the puzzle, you'll feel the containers of anxiety and anger becoming active. And then you find the solution! As you do, do you feel a flash or a sensation that may remind you of a wave going through your torso, from your back to your forehead? That is the boost that we are discussing here. Notice, too, how the containers of anxiety and anger immediately turn off as the boost shoots through your torso. You feel satisfaction—lesser or greater—from solving the clue. But pay careful attention not so much to the additional push itself as to how your mind sent it. And do not try to dissect its mechanism—that normally takes a couple of years, and you do not need to study this mechanism in order to use it. All you need is to identify the boost's trigger and how your mind pulls it. Once you think you've detected what makes the additional push go off, take another of the crossword puzzle's clues and try to intentionally send the push *before* you find the solution. Do you feel the same sort of satisfaction that came from solving the previous clue? If you do, congratulations! Situations may and do differ from each other, but the boost is always nearly the same—the only aspect of it that can vary is how forceful the additional push is.

**Exercise: Using the Boost to Turn Any Emotion into Satisfaction**

From the example described above, you can see that an additional push can be added at any point during any situation. It is easier, however, for a beginner to do this exercise with a push that is already in progress. For instance, suppose you are about to have a job interview, and you are worried. Because this interview is imaginary, you can observe and memorize how the push takes place, distract yourself with another mental image, and then restart the imaginary interview situation, giving the boost to the initial push right when it starts again. Giving the push a boost feels like a small thrust from your back, which your torso guides to your forehead along the same pathway that the initial push took, but the trick is that the boost and the push need to occur nearly simultaneously. Because you naturally do this fairly complex trick on regular basis, you can fairly easily identify it within a situation in which it naturally occurs—either one like the example I offered earlier or another situation from your own past.

When you give the initial push a boost, your feeling of worry should either partially or completely disappear. The degree of your emotional response's modification depends on the force of the boost. If your boost is powerful enough to make the push pass through your entire body and reach the lower forehead, then the only feeling that will be left is that of satisfaction, as if the interview had already taken place.

In real life, you may not have a chance to react to the initial push, particularly if the situation that you want to alter is important to you. Your success with intervening in the push from the previous exercises and the observation of the natural occurrence of the boost (when you recognized the person you thought you had just met or when you found a solution to the problem) should give you a solid foundation to produce a boost later in the situation that has already started.

Try influencing the initial push and then producing an additional push on various situations from your memory. Do your best to achieve the maximum relief—that is, when the emotional response dissipates completely and you feel satisfaction that comes from the achieved goal. When by boosting the push from your back you are able to turn almost any pattern of feelings into satisfaction, you can expect achieving the same result in real-life situations. Start with the situations whose outcomes are not very important to you, gradually taking on progressively more serious situations.

## Technique 3: Redirecting the Push along an Alternative Route

The basis for the technique I call "redirecting the push along an alternate route" also occurs naturally. A few years back, Danni, the eight-year-old son of an acquaintance of mine, was trying to learn how to ride a skateboard. The poor boy kept falling—at times hard—on the pavement, but he continued trying. When you try something and you are unsuccessful at it over and over again, you begin to develop a greater disappointment with every failure. Danni was no different, but he had a natural ability to persevere. Or, to put it simply, he was stubborn.

Observing Danni's body language, you could see the waves of pain, disappointment, and anger surging through the boy's body and, consequently, his mind. You could see how his body adopted a specific muscle tension, particularly visible in his stiffened neck and upper back. At first, Danni's facial expression showed his stubborn resolve whenever he fell and had to fight off disappointment to get back up and try riding the skateboard again, but after several unsuccessful attempts, that stubborn facial expression became constant. The face of stubbornness is always the same: a lowered forehead that does not allow its bearer to look up. This facial expression, along with the increased neck and back tension, gives the push from the back an additional route to reach the forehead, ensuring that all the mind's and body's efforts are funneled toward achieving the set goal. By adopting this expression and pose, Danni successfully deactivated his natural tendency to listen to his feelings or reset his goal. The only feeling that remained active was anger.

Anger is an essential ingredient of stubbornness. (Danni may not have seemed angry, but if you had tried to stop him from trying to ride that untamable skateboard, you would have found out what a real rage is.) Anger is only a problem for people who are naturally stubborn, however. When stubbornness is intentionally produced, anger locks in the goal that you want to accomplish, and the whole mindset becomes surprisingly flexible and obedient.

While stubbornness is rarely praised—and it is often referred to as hardheadedness—using your stubbornness is one of the most effective techniques for shutting down feelings. Yes, stubbornness is frequently a cause for foolish behavior, but that is when it occurs naturally. When you learn to summon your hardheadedness at will, stubbornness gives you exceptional self-control. Admittedly, this technique is among my absolute favorites.

**Getting to Know Your Stubbornness**

Try to recall a time from your past when you were able to accomplish something just because you were stubborn—whether it was climbing a tree, skiing down a steep hill, or beating the daylights out of a bully who was taunting you. As you recollect the situation, pay careful attention to how your mind forms your stubborn state.

As usual, a mental image excites certain feelings strongly enough to trigger a push from your back, and the push goes off toward your lower forehead. But notice that the push does not follow its regular pathway, forward and then upward. When you feel that the push is about to start, you instinctively tense up your back and neck, while lowering your forehead—the pose a stubborn bull takes! Your mind and body change your posture to give the push an alternate route: to go up your back and then forward, along the curved and tilted neck, thus bypassing all containers of feelings. You do experience some other emotions (besides anger) while you are being stubborn, but those feelings did not interfere with your mindset. That's because the push from your back takes a detour around all the containers of emotions and directs itself straight to your goal. Try to memorize how this state of being stubborn feels in your body; it is always the same.

## Exercise: Being Stubborn . . . on Purpose

As usual, you should begin practicing using situations from your past. For this exercise, you will need to reimagine situations in which you failed to follow through, introducing a greater degree of stubbornness to your mindset than you were able to do in the original real-life situation. You need to be able to raise the level of stubbornness to the level that Danni possessed when he struggled with the skateboard. If you were to continue to practice this mental exercise, it would be enough to ensure the successful accomplishment of your goal if it were to repeat itself in real life, but in the meantime, let us make the exercise more tangible.

Try the following exercise: Sit upright on a stool or the edge of a chair, and stay motionless for a certain period, keeping your stubbornness active. You will have to decide for yourself the length of time you should sit, but if you've never done anything of this sort before, then ten minutes should suffice. The purpose of this exercise is to get to the point where you find it difficult to stay still but to have you remain motionless despite your urge to move, relying solely on your stubbornness to maintain the pose. As you continue practicing, increase the length of this exercise, pushing the limits of your innate self-control further and further, every time staying in one position for the amount of time you've set for yourself in advance.

As your training progresses, your stubbornness will become more stable and reliable, and you will be able to apply it to real-life situations. Begin with the chores that you really hate doing, and then little by little use it in situations that are more important to you. For instance, suppose you have a dental appointment, but you really do not want to go. Just make the decision to keep that appointment—do not even bother convincing yourself by reasoning why it is important to see your dentist—and turn on your stubbornness. Any emotions that are not part of the decision that you made will resume their circulation in your mind, but you will feel indifferent toward those emotions; they will not bother you anymore. The crucial point to remember is that you should *never fight the feeling that you dislike*; just do what you decided to do, and leave the task of shutting down the unwanted emotions to your stubbornness.

## Technique 4: Controlling the Push Using Facial Expressions

Picture a man who is running as fast as he can to catch a train that is about to leave the station. I am sure you have no difficulty imagining the man's facial expression. It perfectly conveys the emotional pattern that the man is experiencing. But how can you imagine that expression if you do not even know the man or his face? You can do it because the facial expression will be almost the same for anyone who is about to miss his or her train. The only difference is that the intensity of the emotional response may be lesser or greater, thus making the accompanying facial expression more faint or exaggerated. But who is that facial expression for? It seems to appear on people's faces regardless of whether there are other people around, and the person on whose face this expression appears seems to be too preoccupied with the task at hand—catching the train!—to worry about what his face looks like. Well, the reason why the facial expression is needed in this and any other situation is because the facial expression itself is an integral part of the Goal Setting process.

Stand or sit in front of a mirror, and, observing your reflection, think of a few emotionally charged situations from your past. Do you see how your facial expressions change as you recall different memories? When you are observing yourself in the mirror, however, your facial expressions do not switch as dramatically as they do in normal everyday life. That is because just by watching yourself, you've already set a different goal—that is, to observe the changes in your facial expressions—that competes with the goals you are remembering. You may think that if goal setting is so sensitive, then intentionally modifying it should not be a problem. Well, there is certain ring of truth about that. If you are aware of the changing facial expressions when you are seeing your face in the mirror, you immediately influence the situation from your memory by pushing it deeper in your mind. For instance: Do you feel how a person who is smiling or grinning at you quickly affects your emotional state? Well, you will be influencing your own emotional pattern the same way by looking at your own reflection. If you focus more squarely on the mental images that you are trying to summon and pay attention to the facial expressions in your reflection only with your peripheral vision, you should be able to keep the problem of influencing the expressions that appear on your face under control. But notice that your memories come and go as complex structures. Among other aspects, they include at least the following: the mental image, the emotional response, and the facial expression. This means that in order to alter the emotional response to those memories—and the same goes for real-life situations—you need to know how to split that complex structure apart.

Try the following exercise: While standing or sitting in front of a mirror, recall a situation that made you feel angry. You should see your facial expression become angry. Now distract yourself with other thoughts for a moment, so that the anger is not on your mind anymore, and then think about the same anger-provoking situation again. But this time, do not let your face express anger; just retain whatever facial expression you'd had before you tried to make yourself angry. Do you feel what is going on? The situation that triggers your anger is on your mind, but your anger is unstable: it appears for an instant, but then it dissipates. The reason for this is that you set a goal a moment before you form an emotional response, and the forces that keep your goal alive function as the backbone of your emotional reaction. In other words, you experience feelings only when you have a personal interest in either a real or imaginary situation.

## Getting to Know the Relationship between the Push and Facial Expressions

As we have already discussed, certain mental or real-life images excite your feelings. When the intensity of these feelings is high enough, then the push from your back goes off. The push is always aimed at your lower forehead; on its way to that destination, it presses the containers of the excited feelings between the front and the back of your body, making these feelings stronger and more stable. But notice: while your mind reacts to images—real life or imaginary—your body does not distinguish mental images on the emotional level; only your mind does that. To trigger a reaction from your body, your mind translates even the most complex mental image into an emotional state and then into a facial expression. And also note that what matters most in this phenomenon is not the whole facial expression, but how it affects the middle of your lower forehead. The rest of your facial expression only fine-tunes the movements of the skin of the center of your lower forehead—movements of your mouth, nostrils, eyebrows, and scalp can move the skin between and a little above your eyebrows in all possible directions. You can observe how sensitive the feedback mechanism between the forehead and the push is if you let your mind do its translation, while you manipulate the mental images that appear in the mind's eye. To illustrate how that works, let us consider the following example:

You have an appointment across town, and because it's a lovely day you decide to walk. At one point on your journey, you see a gateway ahead, and it looks as if you'll have to pass through it to reach your destination. Because the gate appears to be wide open, you have no doubts that you can easily go through. Then, as you are getting closer, the gate suddenly swings, leaving only a narrow passage. Do you feel how your speed and the determination in your step immediately decrease? If you observe carefully, you'll notice that the way you are moving has changed because your back has changed the push that sets your goal and propels you toward it. But now the gate opens wide, again. Do you feel how the push from your lower back once again becomes more forceful? And then things change again: the gate swings shut, and you hear what sounds like a lock clicking. Do you feel frustrated? And do you feel how the push from your lower back stops and then sets a different goal—to approach the gate and to see if there's anyone around who can open it. The push that was supposed to deliver you to your destination has become inactive, for now.

When you first see the open gate, you reassess your goal, which has already been set, and modify it to include passage through the gate. Then, as the gate narrows, widens, and then closes, your mind continues to reformat your goal, and the push from your back rapidly changes. The effect that your facial expressions—or, rather, the shifts of the skin on your forehead—have on the push from your back is almost identical to the effect that mental or real-world images have on the push.

## Exercise: Turning Off Feelings Using a Facial Expression

On the one hand, to break the connection between feelings and facial expressions requires a considerable effort, but, on the other, you will usually need only one facial expression to accomplish it: the facial expression of satisfaction.

As you probably remember, you experience satisfaction when you achieve your goal and your feelings related to that goal disappear. This means that no matter what your goal has been or how complex your emotional state was, the facial expression that indicates satisfaction to your body and mind will be the same.

The facial expression of satisfaction is fairly simple—it is a subtle smile. What you need to memorize is not how it looks, but *how you feel* this facial expression, because the sensation of the expression quickly influences the push from the back—after all, this is how it naturally occurs.

You can easily identify the facial expression of satisfaction and the sensations related to it if you remember one of your most important achievements in life. It is better if the achievement that you are thinking of was really a big deal to you, because accomplishment of a big goal gives you a greater satisfaction, and that makes a more effective facial expression. Carefully study the sensations of your facial expression of that satisfaction. Do not forget that the crucial part of your facial expression is the middle of your lower forehead—the rest is secondary to our purpose here.

While standing or sitting in front of a mirror, imagine that you are being offered a food that you hate. You find neither its look nor taste appealing in the least, but its smell alone makes your skin crawl and your stomach turn. But you are expected to eat it!

Can you feel how a grimace is appearing on your face? Well, make it stop! You do not want to offend anybody, right? Try to keep the expression of satisfaction on your face. (You will have a chance to throw that unappetizing dish out, I promise.) Your feelings of aversion and disgust will flare up and quickly dissipate, because the facial expression has precedence for the push, and since your face expresses satisfaction, the expression that comes from disintegrating feelings, the feelings of aversion and disgust will remain unstable.

The most difficult part in this exercise is to prevent your facial expression from switching. Even a slight attempt to change—a subtle twitch, even—is enough for a new emotional state to set in. So make sure that your facial expression does not change even a tiny bit, and you will find this technique to be highly effective.

## Summary

The vast majority of your feelings are very short-lived. Your mind, however, has a mechanism that makes certain emotions incredibly stable, making them seem fresh for many years or even an entire lifetime. Whenever you want to do something but circumstances hold you back, preventing you from achieving your goal, you feel irritated. That irritation exposes that phenomenon, which we call *Goal Setting*, and it works like this:

During any given day, you see a myriad of mental images. Only a few of those images excite feelings in you. Even fewer mental pictures excite emotions strong enough to trigger a push from the back, which is always directed toward the center of your lower forehead—the place where you see *all your mental images,* the mind's eye—thus continuously and physically pressing on the containers of feelings and making your emotions stable in relation to a given mental image. Because we study how to control our feelings through observation, we to use our memory and imagination to discern the different stages of Goal Setting. (The only reason you remember certain situations is because of Goal Setting's involvement.) To identify the useful phases of the mechanism of Goal Setting, you can divide any memory into a mental image, the push from your back, and a facial expression. While you can intervene in and influence Goal Setting in any phase, in this book we look at four effective techniques for altering this process. These techniques are (1) halting the push from the back, (2) giving the push from the back a boost, (3) redirecting the push along an alternate route, and (4) controlling the push via facial expressions.

Recalling situations in which you regretted your actions helps you understand the first technique. There are two possible approaches to this technique: one using a dummy goal and the other using your inner sight. When using a dummy goal—which can be anything that you enjoy picturing yourself doing—you need to keep it firmly in your mind's eye and not let your focus switch to other thoughts that bother you, by simply ignoring them. You don't really ignore them, however. You only keep your mind believing that you direct your actions toward accomplishing the desired goal that you see in your mind's eye, while doing things that you have to do.

The alternative approach doesn't require a goal and works as follows: The mental image of the situation that you would rather forget appears in your mind's eye. If you look at that image, that is if you *look up*, you will trigger a push from your back and thus stabilize your emotional reaction to the mental image. This is similar to what happens when you are pondering something important, looking for a solution: at first, you look down, allowing numerous thoughts to spin fast in your mind. When you recognize the right idea, you look up, thus pinning that particular thought to your mind's eye. If you are unhappy with your find, you lower your eyes, and your mind begins to spin again, carrying the unsatisfactory mental image away with it. Since looking up stabilizes a given mental image and the emotional response that's related to it, then keeping your inner sight directed downward will leave them unstable, and your fast-revolving mind will quickly take them away. The best situations in which to practice this technique are when you're faced with chores that you hate doing. By halting the push, you'll be able to accomplish the chores without being bothered by the negative emotions.

You can also eliminate unwanted feelings if you give a forming emotional response (or an emotional reaction that has already been formed) an additional boost. This phenomenon takes place naturally whenever you are trying to solve a problem and a solution suddenly comes to your mind; when that happens, you feel another push from your back, which alters your emotional pattern from frustration to satisfaction. You can try this technique out using a crossword puzzle, but make sure that the clues to the puzzle are easy for you.

Redirecting the push along an alternate route is known as stubbornness, and you can reproduce it intentionally. First identify the forward-and-down head-tilt, as well as the mindset that accompanies it, from situations from your past in which you acted stubbornly. Then recall a situation in which, for whatever reason, you gave up trying. Reproduce your stubbornness while you're thinking about such a situation, and follow through with whatever it was that you wanted to accomplish—as you wish you had—leaving it to your stubbornness to shut down the emotions that compelled you to behave in a way you didn't want to. Sitting still for increasingly longer periods while keeping the stubborn state of mind can be a very useful exercise for developing a solid command of your stubbornness. You should also try to keep the stubborn mental state as you do your regular chores—particularly those that you hate doing.

Mental images guide your mind, but not your body. Your mind translates your body's emotional responses into facial expressions, thus causing the push from your back to stabilize a particular pattern of feelings. To practice the technique of controlling the push through facial expression, you will need to train yourself to keep the same facial expression—that of satisfaction—whenever your emotional reaction changes. The facial expression of satisfaction is a subtle smile, and the best place to practice it is in front of a mirror, remembering various, progressively more emotionally charged situations. If your smile does not change—not even a tiny bit—then your unwanted feelings will quickly disintegrate.

# CHAPTER 5: EMOTIONS AND THE SECOND BREATH

Once while on vacation, I witnessed the following scene: A little boy, about seven years old, was playing in a river, waist-deep in the water a short distance from the shore. The child's mother was lying a few feet away on the sandy beach, reading a book. At one point, the boy reached for something he saw in the water, slipped, and fell in, head first. His mom lifted her head and, not able to see her son, jumped up and ran into the water. She began combing the bottom of the river with her arms, and in just four swings, she found the boy. The woman grabbed him and pulled him out of the water and onto the beach. She smacked the child's upper back a couple of times with the palm of her hand, and the boy started coughing. The speed and efficiency of her movements were astounding! She did all this in less than a minute. Several people had gotten up and were going to help, but the mother handled everything herself, while staying eerily calm, before anybody managed to react. She held her crying son in her arms, while her eyes sparkled in the sun, still full of shock.

The influx of energy that made her actions so wonderfully coordinated and effective came from a dedicated reservoir from which all emotions borrow energy—a process that is easy to observe when your feelings become unusually strong. Let's identify how our minds and bodies tap into this reservoir.

Suppose you are going to take a bus somewhere, and, while walking to the bus station, you see that the bus is at the gate. You can see the last passenger in line boarding, and you suddenly realize that the bus is about to depart, but you still have a fair distance to go to reach the bus! So you suddenly find yourself running as fast as you can, and when you jump through the bus's still-open door, even though you're gasping and lightheaded, you feel a great satisfaction. That satisfaction results from the disintegration of the feelings associated with your goal of reaching the bus before it left. Those emotions were mainly anxiety and anger. You were worried because the bus might have left without you, and your anger propelled you forward in your race to catch the bus. (To test whether anger was actually involved, imagine yourself missing the bus. Do you feel anger? You most likely do. This is the emotion that catapulted you forward, but you experience the sensations that you recognize as anger only when the bus has taken off without you.)

Your goal was to get somewhere, and the bus was a means to do it. But notice that your goal did not seem nearly as urgent before you saw that the bus was about to leave. So how did your desire to accomplish what you had planned suddenly become so strong? To observe what happened, picture the situation again, and notice the change in your torso (and, consequently, your emotions) at the moment you saw the bus and realized that you might not make it. Do you feel your pelvis tilting backward, tightening your entire torso in the direction of your forehead? This adjustment allows the push that helps to form your goal and to initialize your actions to flow directly from your back to your lower forehead, thus excluding any other thoughts or feelings. At the same time, your muscles tense up, and your desire to get on that bus compels you to take instant action!

## Natural Occurrence of the Phenomenon behind the Technique

This mechanism comes into play every time circumstances force you to squeeze your feelings' containers to accomplish a set goal sooner. But it is important to point out that this mechanism also works in the opposite direction. In other words, you can use the mechanism to *weaken* any emotion to the point of its disappearance—and this is why we're discussing it here.

The easiest way to observe how the same reservoir that can lend you a burst of energy can, in a different situation, also absorb it is to empty this reservoir, at least a little, and then to watch it fill up again. To see how this happens, let's use the chasing-the-bus example again, but focus on a different stage of the experience.

Suppose you've run to catch the bus, and when you finally catch up with it, you find yourself out of breath and gasping for air. Observe what your body and mind instinctively do to regain your composure. The first thing you do is to stop whatever you've been doing that has made you tired—in this case, running. You stop expending your energy, and your mind reassesses your current condition.

If you observe yourself carefully, you'll notice that your consciousness measures your degree of exhaustion by the state of your lower torso. If you are only moderately tired—as you would be after chasing the bus—then, once you stop running, you give yourself a chance to catch your breath. You may feel the need to sit down. Suppose, on the other hand, that you've had a very tiring day at work and are utterly exhausted. In such a case, you might feel an irresistible urge to *lie* down. What sensations play the crucial role in letting you know how much rest you need or want? Your decision has to do with how stable the area right above your pelvis feels, particularly your lower back.

The sensation that I want you to pay special attention to is the feeling that your breathing is not reaching your lower abdomen. After you run for a while, your breathing becomes heavy. Even though you're inhaling more strongly than you usually do, you feel that you are not getting enough air. Normally, when you breathe, you feel the urge to inhale, and with every breath you take, you feel satisfaction—that's how you know you've inhaled enough. When you are out of breath, however, this satisfaction comes more slowly, and you pant. Observing your torso, you can feel how running and other strenuous physical activities involve many muscles in your body. When so many muscles flex at the same time but don't fully relax, they absorb much of the energy and even the movements that come from the inhalation. As a result, when you draw in a breath, it doesn't go all the way down to your lower abdomen.

Essentially, the technique that we're about to discuss in this chapter involves fooling your mind into thinking that the real emotion that you're trying to turn off is located in the lower abdomen rather than in the feeling's container or containers. When your mind's attention shifts from the container to the lower abdomen, you'll no longer experience that unwanted emotion. The lower abdomen simply has this power to deactivate any feeling, but in order to summon this power, your breath absolutely needs to reach your lower abdomen. Let's look at this mechanism more closely.

Suppose you've been doing something more strenuous than just chasing a bus. Say you've been unloading a truck for several hours without a break, and you're feeling very tired. You feel that you've just got to stop working and sit down. Partly, the problem remains the same: too many muscles are constricting at the same time, and, to support their tension, these muscles attract and disperse the energy that comes with your inhalation. After such labor, your mind's solution to this problem is to make you stay still.

You might argue that after hours of physical labor, it is perfectly normal to feel this way. That might be so, but did you ever feel so emotionally drained that you had to lie down? Was your state similar to the physical exhaustion? Actually, any persistent sensation drains your energy; a stronger sensation can do it sooner, while a milder one takes longer. Take, for example, the sensation of pain. I am sure you can imagine (or remember) how tiring it is to have a toothache for a whole day. What if it lasts for a couple of days straight? You will feel exhausted. When you work hard physically, you spend your energy working. But where does your energy go after a long period of stress or pain? You spend it on emotions or suffering.

Let's say you've had a lot of paperwork to do, and it has taken you fourteen hours to complete it. You've met your deadline—finishing the paperwork at one o'clock in the morning—and you are beat. In this case, not nearly as many containers have been activated, and the sensations that you are experiencing are different from those following physical labor, but your mind interprets these sensations, too, as meaning that you are tired. You feel as if you've spent a lot of energy, but you know that you were just sitting at your desk the entire day. This kind of work-related exhaustion is very common. Even if you enjoy your work and like the people with whom you work, you'll feel tired after a day of work.

It doesn't matter whether the feelings you experience are positive or negative—they all require energy to exist. No matter the reason for your fatigue, you will feel weakness in your lower torso—more so in the lower back, as if it no longer has the power to support your upper body. Now, as you rest, either sitting or lying down, you have the chance to observe how your body recovers its energy resources. Your breathing reaches deeper into the abdomen and seems to adhere to something closer to the back, a little bit below the area in which the initial push originates. When you are really out of breath, your inhalations cannot grab onto anything in the lower torso, and that sensation makes you gasp for more air. And until the inhalations do take hold, you'll still feel exhausted. But once the inhalation penetrates through the lower abdomen to the lower back, you'll begin to feel more satisfaction and more strength with every breath that you take. Again, your strength comes from the sensation that your lower torso, particularly your lower back, behind your lower abdomen, has become firmer and more stable.

With practice, you will be able to develop greater skill in drawing inhalations to your lower torso through your lower abdomen. As your lower torso soaks up more drawn-in breaths, you'll feel more energetic. You'll be able to reproduce the sensation of a firmer, more stable lower back at will and to maintain it so that it doesn't disappear. Does that mean you won't ever get tired? Well, no. You will still get tired, but not nearly as soon as you normally would.

This power to direct your inhalations to the lower torso, making it feel firm and stable, is a prerequisite to using the technique discussed below; otherwise, your lower torso won't have the strength to turn off a feeling, which essentially relies on your lower torso's ability to produce the sensation of "grabbing" inhalations. To ensure that it has the necessary energy, you must train yourself to breathe more deeply, so that your breath reaches your lower abdomen most of the time. You can start training by setting twenty minutes in the morning and twenty in the evening during which you either sit or stand still and breathe with your lower abdomen. When you become comfortable breathing with your lower abdomen, begin implementing this practice in your everyday life. Pay attention to the postures in which you find it difficult to breathe this way while running errands or working, because those are the positions that you'll want to use as you continue to practice. Also try to notice those postures in which lower abdominal breathing comes easily and turn to them whenever you get tired of breathing this way, because the goal is to train yourself to breathe *effortlessly* with your lower abdomen. Your mind and body want to turn to it as a way to relax, so finding the positions in which this breathing requires barely any effort is crucial. As you practice breathing in the positions in which your inhalation doesn't reach your lower abdomen very well, the lower abdominal breathing will become progressively easier to do.

## Essential Components of the Technique

As you practice switching off unwanted emotions using this technique, you'll find that your success will depend, in part, on the way you normally breathe and how greatly you need to modify that, on your body type, on how emotional you are, on which emotions have precedence to your mind, and so on. No matter what your personality is like, however, there are a few components that are crucial to the successful outcome of your efforts.

To be successful at turning off a feeling, this technique must have the following three components: (1) the muscular tension in your lower abdomen has to be a tiny bit greater than the muscular tension in and around the container of the unwanted feeling; (2) your breathing has to be of a higher quality than the breathing associated with the unwanted feeling; and (3) your pelvis has to align with the container of the feeling that you wish to turn off. Let's consider each of these components individually.

## Intensity of Muscle Tension

In the chapter on the activating breath, we discussed the several breathing techniques that allow you to reach the various containers of emotion. Here, we're going to use only the technique of breathing with the lower abdomen. To remind you, briefly, how this breathing technique works: You flex the muscles of your abdominal wall during exhalation, pulling it inward and thus pushing the air out of your lungs. To inhale, you simply release the muscle tension, and the abdominal wall returns to its original position. Do note, however, that when performing this technique you shouldn't release the muscle tension completely, because it's crucial that your lower abdomen be able to create and maintain greater muscular tension than any of the containers can. The size of this area and its natural dominance over *all* the containers make this possible.

As you'll recall, the lower abdomen is the area of sexual desire, and it has a natural ability to access and influence any container of feelings. Among the approaches described in this book, this technique is one of the most effective at stopping unwanted feelings, essentially because the technique "highjacks" the area of sexual desire, which already has the power to modify any given emotional state. Its execution, however, requires another specialized skill: higher-quality breathing. So let's take a look at that, next.

## Higher-Quality Breathing

Every feeling you normally experience comes with impurities, that is, every breath contains small failures to sustain that feeling. These failures last a mere instant each, but there are at least a few of them within a single breath. These impurities manifest themselves in greater or lesser irregularities in the flow of each and every inhalation or exhalation, making you lose your emotional state for a very, very brief moment and then immediately restore it. To see what I mean, think about something that makes you joyful—an upcoming vacation, maybe. As you enjoy this thought, carefully observe your breathing—paying close attention to its inconsistencies, the interruptions in the flow of breath. Your inhalations play a greater role in your breathing's rhythm, because inhalations are responsible for maintaining your emotional state. As you continue to observe, you'll notice that *none* of your breaths is consistent. At multiple points during a single inhalation, as well as during an exhalation, the flow deviates from the initial momentum and then restores that momentum a moment later. If that deviation from the flow is too great or lasts too long, you'll lose the momentum, and your thoughts will veer away from your future vacation and toward some other subject, changing your feelings in the process. If you take dozens of feelings and observe the consistency of the inhalations associated with them, you'll be able to identify the average deviation level of your emotions. To have the power to turn off an emotion, you'll need to reduce the inconsistencies in your breathing from the lower abdomen. To put it another way: you'll have to improve the quality of your breathing.

## Pelvic Alignment

Suppose you're walking down a street, and you think you hear somebody cheerfully calling your name. You turn around to see who is calling you, but you don't see anybody you know. People are passing you by, and no one seems to recognize you, either.

When you thought you heard someone calling you, it attracted your interest. The feeling of interest is located in the center of your chest, meaning that it is a type of joy. But when you turn around and don't see anyone you recognize, your interest deactivates. As soon as your mind decides that there's no goal to set—because the goal would be tied to the person who called out your name, and your emotional reaction would be set accordingly—your mind's attention shifts away from your forehead. Now your lower abdomen starts to feel stronger. Despite its increase in tension, it calms down your excitement by attracting your attention to its movement. There is only one inhalation that turns off most of your interest, and right before that inhalation, your pelvis tilts down and forward—as opposed to up and backward, as when you were chasing a bus—aligning with the container of joy. You will probably feel some remainder of this joy for a little while—in the form of a question to yourself, "Who could that have been?"—but essentially, the feeling is gone. (The emotion would dissolve completely if you were to adjust the muscle tension involved in your lower abdominal breathing to slightly exceed the tension of muscles around the active container of joy.)

This example illustrates the technique that we'll discuss below in relation to each of the emotions. It takes some observational skill to catch this mechanism in action, and it usually takes about four months of two-hour training daily to develop the skill needed to use this technique effectively.

**Joy**

Every time Laura is stressed, she wants to eat. Whenever Laura is relaxed, she also wants to eat. When she is among friends, she doesn't mind eating, either. When Laura is all alone, she thinks about having a snack. Laura is lucky that she has a fast metabolism, but she is a little overweight. She wants to stop overeating, but eating seems to provide a reliable comfort. She often tries dieting but soon returns to her old dietary habits.

You're may be asking, *So, where's the joy here?* The answer is that eating gives Laura a feeling of comfort, which is a form of joy.

# The Natural Occurrence of Joy

Imagine yourself in Laura's situation, or bring to mind a habitual behavior that you tend to engage in frequently simply because you like it—that is, your habit gives you a feeling of comfort. Whenever you feel the urge to turn to your habit for comfort, there must be something that happened just prior to the appearance of that urge that gives you a greater degree of discomfort than you're used to, so your mind feels compelled to look for ways to calm itself down. When it finds a behavior that works, you feel joy—and you can tell that it's joy you feel because the container of joy becomes activated. You feel the center of your chest more pronouncedly than you usually do, and that sensation attracts and holds your attention as long as you're doing whatever it is that calms you down.

Let's see, though, how we can intervene in joy's formation using the technique of breathing with the lower abdomen—and what happens to the emotional state when we do so.

**Exercise: Disruption of Joy**

Again imagine yourself either in Laura's shoes or just before you begin indulging in whatever habit you find comforting, and observe what happens to your breathing. It becomes even more irregular and inconsistent than normal and there are brief lapses from the initial momentum of each breath, because discomfort always increases the degree of deviation from the smooth breath flow that (ideally) sustains an emotional state. When you begin doing whatever it is that typically calms you down—whether eating or something else—you can feel your breathing smooth out, and you begin to feel calmer.

Your inhalations are still far from perfect, however, because the discomfort is still there in your mind. As unpleasant as discomfort is, it emphasizes weaknesses in your emotional state, causing you engage in bad habits.

Paradoxically, to break your bad habit, you'll have to disrupt the formation of the joy, or comfort, that that habit ordinarily brings you. To do this, begin breathing with your lower abdomen, trying to keep your exhalations and inhalations more consistent than the breathing associated with the joy. Because breathing with the lower abdomen requires effort during the exhalation and because the inhalation has a tendency to mimic the quality of your exhalation, you need to make the air flow exceptionally smooth during both taking in and letting out each breath. As you adjust your breathing to the breathing associated with joy, you'll no longer feel comfort from engaging in whatever behavior you've typically used to calm yourself.

You can also, if you wish, destroy the *dis*comfort that triggers your turning to your habit. To do that, you need to continue smoothing out the flow of your breath until you feel that your discomfort is going away. Whatever the mechanism is, the discomfort in this emotional pattern is naturally tied up with joy, that is, the feeling of comfort, and so the deactivation of joy will have a destructive effect on the associated discomfort—an effect that you'll witness first-hand when you try this exercise.

**Aversion**

Dave is a computer programmer, and he needs to take a certification test, but every time he tries to study, he finds it difficult to concentrate. He feels bored by the material that he needs to read, understand, and memorize. He tries to force himself to focus on the text, but his mind keeps drifting off.

## The Natural Occurrence of Aversion

Boredom is a kind of aversion. Picture yourself in Dave's shoes or think of a similar situation in which you had to do something boring, and observe the sensations in your torso that make you realize that you're experiencing boredom. The most prominent of those sensations is the twirling from side to side that you feel around the center of your chest, which means that the container of aversion is active, showing that boredom is a manifestation of aversion.

## Exercise: Disruption of Aversion

Continue to think about the same situation, so that the feeling of aversion stays active, and begin to adjust the tension of your breathing with your lower abdomen until your mind interprets the sensation appearing in your lower abdomen as a slightly stronger aversion. (For reasons that are unknown—to me, at least—when your lower abdominal breathing achieves a tension similar to the tension that naturally sustains a feeling in its container, the sensation in your lower abdomen takes precedence over the actual feeling, making your mind lose the emotion that you are choosing to turn off.) You can detect the right tension when it seems to you that the container of aversion and your lower abdomen resonate with each other; they kind of come together. When you've accomplished this, focus your efforts on the consistency of your lower abdominal breathing. It's crucial at this point to align your pelvis with the container so that every inhalation associated with your aversion reaches to your lower abdomen. As you make the breathing increasingly flawless, you'll feel your lower abdomen winning the tug-of-war with the container of aversion. At that point, the container of aversion will abruptly turn off, and you'll become aware of your lower abdomen and an influx of energy in your chest and face, which feels like a warm wave washing over your upper body. Now, if you think again about the situation that triggered your aversion, you won't feel your aversion anymore. It will, however, appear if you think about a different aversion-provoking situation, but if you do this exercise on several dozen such situations, you'll become skilled enough to deactivate your aversion whenever it interferes with your ability to do something that must be done.

**Sadness**

Rose got married when she was twenty, and soon after she gave birth to the first of her two children. Now Rose is forty, both her children are away at college, and when she looks back on her life, Rose regrets that she got married and had children at such a young age. "I could have done something interesting with my life," she thinks.

While Rose cannot turn back time, she's only forty years old, and she still has plenty of time to do something that she finds interesting. Feeling regretful is useless to her, because regret just clouds her judgment, getting in the way of her embarking on a more rewarding life.

**The Natural Occurrence of Sadness**

Don't forget that what we call *sadness* in this book doesn't mean only the feeling of sadness per se. In fact, don't worry about having to name any emotion you're feeling. Instead, determine which emotion you're experiencing according to which container becomes active while you're feeling that emotion, and use this technique to turn off whatever feeling it is.

To see that regret is a manifestation of sadness, just think about something that you could have done but missed your chance to do, and observe where you experience your regret. Do you feel it in the sides of your chest? You most likely do. Note, too, that sadness has many shades and that each of these shades is distributed either slightly or significantly differently within the container of sadness. That's because every emotion is a unique reflection of a specific situation and will never be identical to any other manifestation of that feeling. This means that the pattern of activation of a feeling's container varies every time.

**Exercise: Disruption of Sadness**

To ensure a good result from this exercise, make sure that your posture is straight. Whenever you experience sadness, you, like anyone else, tend to stoop forward. When you stoop, it becomes more difficult to turn off the container of sadness using your lower abdomen. You need to feel that your breathing reaches your lower abdomen with every breath, so you have the full function of the area of sexual desire at your service.

Think of a situation that triggers your regret, and observe the change in the tension of breathing that accompanies that emotion. Now, match the tension of breathing with your lower abdomen to the muscle tension around the container of sadness until your mind's focus shifts away from the container of sadness and toward the lower abdomen. Once you've achieved that, begin removing irregularities from your breathing. When your inhalation contains fewer inconsistencies than the natural breathing, the container of sadness deactivates in relation to the given situation.

**Anxiety**

Simon experiences strong anxiety whenever he talks to women. His voice starts to tremble, his hands become clammy, and his stomach rumbles. These symptoms become even more intense if he really likes the woman he's talking with.

Simon's anxiety is, of course, accompanied by sexual desire, but his anxiety alone is the focus of our discussion here. The activation of the area of sexual desire makes Simon's anxiety stronger and sharper, something that active sexual desire can do to any emotion.

This means that if he just turns off anxiety's container, his problem will be resolved.

**The Natural Occurrence of Anxiety**

At the very beginning of anxiety's appearance, the container of anxiety starts to constrict under the pressure created by the surrounding muscles and the weight of the upper body. Even if the pressure is light, you'll feel the sensation of a hole in your solar plexus, which appears almost instantly. If you let the sensation of a hole appear, then it's going to take a lot of effort to restore the container to its dormant state. The best time to interfere in anxiety's formation is therefore during those brief moments when the pressure around the feeling's container is just building up.

Because in real-life situations the pressure builds up and the container constricts within a fraction of a second, and the symptoms of anxiety—such as weakness in the upper abdomen and trembling that quickly spreads all over your body—immediately capture your attention, it's nearly impossible to develop a good technique for disrupting anxiety. Imagination, however, allows you to slow down anxiety's activation enough to identify each of its phases of development. So if you think about an anxiety-provoking situation and immediately experience the sensation of a hole in your solar plexus, distract yourself for a moment, and then run through the same situation again, observing carefully how that sensation of a hole gets formed. The muscles around the container of anxiety tense up, and the sensation of the upper abdomen immediately becomes weak, particularly if your anxiety is intense. You feel as if your upper abdomen can no longer support your upper body. Instinctively, your torso leans a little forward, trying to close the sensation of a gap in your solar plexus. This sensation of decreased muscle tone creates a panic in your mind, which, in turn, causes those anxiety-related symptoms.

The crucial component of taking control over your anxiety is not to let your torso bend forward, because once you do, your access to the lower abdomen becomes limited. Think of a few anxiety-provoking situations, and try to catch the moments before you lean forward. Train yourself to keep your posture straight during the instant when the sensation of a hole is being formed.

**Exercise: Disruption of Anxiety**

Another reason you need to catch the very beginning of feeling worried is because this is the only moment when you can find out the degree of muscle tension that your anxious emotional state produces. You need to adjust your breathing with your lower abdomen to a slightly greater degree of muscle tension than what occurs right before the muscular pressure squeezes the container of anxiety and the whole area feels dissipated. Once you feel that the breathing with your lower abdomen has captured your mind's attention, increase the consistency of breathing within each breath. You should feel your solar plexus filling up with strength again. When you become comfortable in using your breathing to shut down your anxiety, you can do something else with it.

If you get past your anxiety and adjust your breathing further, smoothing out progressively more inconsistencies and irregularities in the inhalations' and exhalations' flow, you'll experience confidence. Remember that there's no container of confidence. If you wish to become comfortably confident, you simply need to deactivate the container of anxiety to a greater degree. Sensation-wise, all you will feel is that the hole no longer forms in the middle of your upper abdomen. The area feels strong and supports your upper body well. That's *all* you need to feel confident. Try it.

After practicing on several dozen worry-inducing situations, you should become comfortable manipulating your anxiety by interfering in the initial stage of its development. Try out your skills on situations as they occur in real life, starting with disrupting mild anxiety and then disrupting increasingly more intense manifestations of this feeling. When you get comfortable with this technique, you can try—if you wish—to turn off anxiety at a later stage in its development. Although it makes sense to disrupt anxiety at the earliest stage of its formation, you may want to try to do it later on, just in a case of emergency. For this, the technique needs no modification; all you need to do is to *not* let your mind's focus adhere to the sensations that it interprets as anxiety, which you can accomplish by grasping and holding your mind's attention with super-refined lower abdominal breathing, but this skill comes automatically with practice.

**Anger**

You've been standing in a long line at the convenience store, when some fellow cuts in front of you! The guy has only two six-packs of beer, so you say nothing, but then the cashier tells him that his credit card has been declined, and the fellow starts to argue, wasting even more of everyone's time. You feel your anger boiling up inside you.

**The Natural Occurrence of Anger**

Anger is a difficult feeling to control, particularly when it's intense. This difficulty is largely due to the change in your body's posture. Notice how your torso arches your ribcage forward to turn on your anger, and you immediately feel the burning sensation that identifies this emotion to your mind. It starts from its two ignition points, whose locations you can clearly feel on the each side of your ribcage whenever you think of an anger-provoking situation, and then quickly fills anger's containers. The greatest problem with anger filling up larger portions of its containers is that when its containers are more than half full, they divide the upper and lower torso, making lower abdominal breathing increasingly difficult. This is why, in a way akin to deactivation of anxiety, you need to observe anger's development in its initial stages. You'll need to become comfortable interfering at those stages in order to be able to disrupt anger as it occurs in real life.

# Exercise: Disruption of Anger

Place yourself mentally back in that same queue, and observe what happens to your emotional state when someone cuts in front of you.

It's crucial to keep your lower abdomen aligned with this arching forward, or your anger will take over your emotional state. What makes this takeover possible is the forward shift of your torso right below the lower edges of the containers of anger. You can prevent this from happening if you (1) keep a straight posture and (2) mimic the ribcage's shift forward with your lower abdomen.

Essentially, the technique for disrupting the emotion remains the same: You need to adjust your lower abdominal breathing until its tension slightly exceeds the tension around the containers of anger. If you do, you'll feel your mind's focus shifting from the containers to the lower abdomen. Because your mid-torso arches a little bit forward, you need to align your lower abdomen with anger's containers by tilting your pelvis more downward and forward than usual. Now, begin eliminating inconsistencies from the flow of your exhalation and inhalation. Once the consistency reaches a certain threshold, the pressure on anger's containers will instantly disappear, and so will your anger.

Because each instance of anger is associated with a particular situation, gaining skill at disrupting anger requires that you repeat the same exercise with a number of anger-provoking situations from your life. To prepare for turning off your anger as the emotion appears in real life, give preference to situations that *typically* trigger your anger. Remember, too, that how well you do this exercise is more important than how many situations you use when practicing.

**Fear**

Heather recently noticed a couple of dark stains in the middle of her living room ceiling, and she's decided to try to get rid of them. She's set up a ladder in the center of the room, and, wet sponge in hand, she climbs up. But as Heather reaches the top, she realizes that she's afraid to let go of the ladder, which she needs to do in order to clean the stains. The situation causes her too much fright, and she climbs back down, trembling and frustrated.

## The Natural Occurrence of Fear

As the muscles around fear's containers constrict and the weight of your upper body ensures steady pressure on the containers, fear spreads from the depth of your upper abdomen and fills up its two containers toward your back. As fear fills its containers, you can feel its increasingly paralyzing effect spreading through your body. If you miss the initial stage of fear's formation, the fear containers become locked, and unlocking them, while possible, takes too much effort.

This locking of the containers is caused by your posture. Your torso arches forward at the level of your upper abdomen—a movement almost identical to the arching of the torso that accompanies anger's formation. In the case of fear, however, the focus of the torso's bending—the place where the crease in the muscles is most pronounced—is located much deeper in the body, near the back wall of the ribcage.

## Exercise: Disruption of Fear

Picture yourself in Heather's situation or think of any situation that has frightened you. As you did with the other feelings, begin by observing the very beginning of your fear's appearance and the moments before your emotional state switches. Then, keeping your back in the same state it is in just prior to fear's appearance, adjust the intensity of your lower abdominal breathing to match the muscular tension around the containers of fear. Once you notice that your mind can't tell where the fear is located—whether in the emotion's containers or in your lower abdomen—begin removing every inconsistency in the flow of your breath with the lower abdomen.

When you become comfortable disrupting fear at the beginning of its formation in many different frightening situations, you can try to disrupt it at later stages of development. The technique remains the same. What determines whether or not you're able to use it at these later stages is your ability to hold your inner focus on the lower abdomen. Remember that the same two factors play the crucial role: (1) a well-adjusted muscular tension in the lower abdomen that slightly exceeds the tension around the container(s) that you wish to deactivate, and (2) fewer inconsistencies in the lower abdominal breathing than in the breathing associated with the unwanted emotion. With practice, you should be able to deactivate the containers of fear with just one inhalation at any stage of its development.

## Disgust

Ted is walking to work, and he sees a group of people ahead, blocking the narrow sidewalk, so he makes a little detour around them, stepping onto a lawn. But it rained hard last night, and the lawn is soaked. Accidentally, Ted steps into a surprisingly deep puddle. His foot gets stuck in the mud and—as if by malicious design!—the mud fills the interior of his shoe as Ted tries to break the suction created by the slimy, sticky muck. "That's great," Ted mumbles to himself. "Now I'll have to spend the whole day at work wearing a wet, dirty shoe."

If you imagine yourself in this situation, you'll very likely experience anger and frustration in addition to disgust, but, please, pay no attention to the other feelings. Focus only on the repulsion that you experience as the cold, wet mud seeps into your shoe.

## The Natural Occurrence of Disgust

The muscles around disgust's single container constrict, and the feeling appears from the ignition point located on the back wall of the container and spreads toward your abdomen. The lower portion of the stomach is right in the middle of the container, and when the container squeezes your stomach, you may have an urge to throw up. Even though the pressure on the container of disgust comes almost exclusively from the tightened muscles around the container, your body stoops a little bit forward, but not because it provides additional pressure on the container. Because of the container's location in the middle of your abdomen, your body can't apply its weight to press on it. Your stooping forward is meant to release the muscle stretch in the abdomen caused by the upright posture. Once you bend forward just a little, the muscles immediately squeeze the container even more, and you instantly feel repulsed by the mud filling your shoe.

## Exercise: Disruption of Disgust

Imagine yourself in a disgust-provoking situation, and, as usual, pay close attention to the very beginning of the emotion's appearance. Chances are—particularly if your disgust is intense—that simply keeping an upright posture may not be enough to disrupt the emotion. To gain greater control over the container's constriction, you may want to arch your mid-abdomen slightly forward to stretch the abdominal muscles around the container a little more. This gives you an opportunity to move your mind's focus to the lower abdomen.

The technique itself is still the same: (1) adjust the tension of your lower abdominal breathing to slightly exceed the muscle tension around the container of disgust, and (2) once the two sensations meld together and become indistinguishable to your mind, start removing inconsistencies from the flow of your breath until you deactivate the container.

As it becomes easy for you to disrupt your disgust at the beginning of its appearance, you can try the same technique to turn the emotion off at later stages. The crucial part of this technique when applied to disgust is to keep your abdominal muscles stretched at all times, because if the muscles surrounding the container of disgust contract, they may go into a spasm, causing you to vomit. If that happens, all your further attempts will be futile.

## Sexual Desire

Harry just started dating Jane, and thinking about her still excites him a lot. Harry, however, has an important test in two days, and he really needs to study. Chances are that Harry doesn't find the material that he ought to be learning nearly as exciting as his thoughts about Jane! Even though aversion plays a significant part in this situation, don't to focus on the aversion here. In a similar real-life situation, you *would* have to turn off your aversion as well as your sexual desire, but that's always done as a separate step (which you already know how to do).

## The Natural Occurrence of Sexual Desire

In a way that's akin to how disgust is formed, sexual desire turns on almost exclusively by means of muscle constriction. The torso still stoops a little forward, but not because it adds the bodyweight to the pressure; it simply decreases the tension of muscles in the lower abdomen, so the muscles would have more flexibility to constrict to various degrees. The constriction of the muscles in the lower part of the abdominal wall creates pressure on the two points—each located about three finger-breadths below your navel and about one-hand width to the each side of the midline. The sexual desire spreads inwardly—from the abdominal wall in the direction of the back—the extent of how far it spreads depends on the degree of sexual excitement.

**Exercise: Disruption of Sexual Desire**

If you imagine yourself in Harry's situation or in any other in which you had to curb your sexual excitement and try using breathing with your lower abdomen to turn off your sexual desire, you will be disappointed. This technique does dilute the feeling, but it also makes it more persistent. Because this technique involves "hijacking" the area of sexual desire to deactivate other feelings, it doesn't work the same way on sexual desire itself.

If you want to apply this technique to turn off your sexual excitement, think of any situation that activates any container(s) of feelings in your body and then adjust your breathing to that feeling. The absolute best killer of sexual excitement is anxiety, so any anxiety-inducing situation will do—or, rather, adjusting lower-abdomen breathing to the intensity of breathing that maintains the anxiety will deactivate your sexual area.

## Summary

The lower abdomen, besides being the area of sexual desire, contains the energy reserve for the entire body. Its function becomes much easier to observe when an emotion becomes unusually intense. It can also absorb energy from any emotion, thus turning it off. This capacity to absorb energy is what the technique discussed in this chapter is all about.

The easiest way to familiarize yourself with how this technique occurs naturally is to tap and spend some of the energy contained in the reservoir of the lower abdomen, because then you can observe how it fills up again.

To use this technique at will, you need to work on breathing with your lower abdomen—the only type of breathing necessary to employ this technique. For its successful application, your lower abdominal breathing has to incorporate three components: (1) the muscle tension in your lower abdomen needs to be greater than the tension of the muscles around the container(s) of the unwanted emotion; (2) the quality of your lower-abdomen breathing needs to be higher than that of the breath that maintains the feeling you want to deactivate; and (3) your pelvis needs to align itself with the container of the feeling that you wish to deactivate.

Any emotion appears because its container is being squeezed by the surrounding muscles. Your mind will naturally shift its focus to your lower abdomen, however, if the muscle tension exceeds that of the area around the container, thus releasing the pressure on the container and turning off the feeling it produces.

Natural breathing always contains inconsistencies. In every breath you take in or let out, the flow of air is irregular, because the intensity of muscle tension fluctuates. Your lower abdominal breathing begins to influence an unwanted emotion when the number of irregularities in the air flow becomes less than the number that occurs in the natural breathing associated with the emotion.

To make this technique work, your inhalations must reach your lower abdomen not only when you're using this technique but as part of your normal breathing, and your lower abdomen needs to be aligned with the feeling's container, so the movement of inhalation can pass through the container and connect it with your lower abdomen in an uninterrupted flow.

Joy has many forms, of which comfort is one. People engage in habitual behaviors because of the comfort they produce, so if you turn off the comfort, the desire to engage in the habit will also disappear. To deactivate any form of joy, adjust the tension of your breathing to match and then slightly exceed the tension of breathing associated with your joy. When your mind starts to confuse the lower abdomen with the container of joy, begin removing irregularities in the flow of your breath, until your mind releases the container of joy and your lower abdomen captures your mind's attention completely.

Aversion, too, comes in a multitude of forms. One of the most common and annoying is boredom. To turn off any form of aversion, adjust your lower abdominal breathing's tension to mimic the breathing associated with the type of aversion that you want to switch off, align your lower torso with the container of aversion, and smooth out the irregularities in your lower abdominal breathing until the feeling disappears.

Stooping, which often accompanies sadness, makes it difficult to align your lower torso with the container of sadness. But if your inhalations reach your lower abdomen, you don't feel the need to stoop. Catching the formation of your sadness early allows you to easily align your lower abdomen with the container of sadness. As you perform this alignment, or even a moment earlier or later, adjust the tension of your breathing so that it slightly exceeds the tension of the breathing that maintains any of the many shades of sadness, and then improve the flow of your breath in your lower abdomen. The heavy sensation of sadness will quickly vanish.

To deactivate anxiety, it's essential to identify the change in breathing's tension at the very beginning of the feeling's appearance. If you miss that early stage of anxiety's activation, turning it off becomes more difficult, because the sensation of the container disappears, and your mind becomes strongly attracted to the sensation of a hole that occupies the middle of your upper abdomen. If you mentally practice controlling anxiety, however, it becomes easy to catch the early phase of anxiety's appearance. Another major difficulty with controlling anxiety involves the tendency to bend forward at the level of anxiety's container, which makes it difficult to align the lower abdomen with the container. The best trick for solving this problem is not to let this stooping forward occur. It's only mildly difficult to interfere with the feeling's formation at the very beginning. The technique itself remains the same: Adjust the tension of your abdominal breathing to match and slightly surpass the tension of breathing that naturally sustains your anxiety, align your lower abdomen with the solar plexus, and smooth out the inconsistencies in the flow of your breath. Your anxiety should be gone within a breath or two.

The difficulty with controlling anger lies in the muscle tension and alignment. Anger's containers become active from points that are close to the upper abdominal surface, and to align your lower torso with this arching forward, you'll need to tilt your pelvis down and forward a little bit more than you do it with other feelings. The muscle tension that maintains anger is often great. Once you align your lower abdomen with the containers, adjust your breathing to match the anger's tension, and reduce irregularities in the breathing's flow. Your anger should turn off within a few inhalations.

To use this technique on your fear, you should avoid letting the fear lock in the containers. The easiest way to prevent this is to observe the moments just prior to fear's appearance and to resist the urge to straighten and arch your back—the movement that accompanies fear's formation. If you manage to prevent the locking of the containers, the rest of the technique is the same as for other feelings (but even easier).

The crucial element in disrupting disgust is to keep the muscles in the middle of your abdomen slightly stretched, because when the feeling of disgust forms, you experience an urge to bend a little bit forward. This bending forward is enough to allow your muscles and the feeling's container to constrict, which can cause vomiting—at which point it's too late to interfere in disgust's activation. As with anger, disgust doesn't increase gradually. The breathing's tension becomes strong with only one inhalation, which you need to adjust your lower abdominal breathing to instantly, but if you continue keeping the middle of your abdomen stretched, you can slow down its progress a little bit.

Disruption of sexual desire works somewhat differently. Because this technique makes use of the area of sexual desire's natural ability to influence all the containers, using it directly on sexual desire will cause the desire to persist instead of shutting it off. The easiest way to deactivate sexual feelings using this technique is to adjust the tension of your lower abdominal breathing to match or slightly exceed that of any other emotion. The best effect can be realized by adjusting your breathing to the tension of anxiety and then smoothing out the irregularities of the flow. Pelvic tilt plays very little role in this application of the technique.

THE END